Photographic Data

Titles in the Technical Pocket Book series

Photographic Chemistry and Processing

Photographic Data

Photographic Imaging and Electronic Photography

Photographic Lenses and Optics

Photographic Printing and Enlarging

Photographic Technology and Image Science

Photographic Data

Series editor: Sidney F Ray

Focal Press
An imprint of Butterworth-Heinemann Ltd
Linacre House, Jordan Hill, Oxford OX2 8DP

A member of the Reed Elsevier plc group

OXFORD LONDON BOSTON
MUNICH NEW DELHI SINGAPORE SYDNEY
TOKYO TORONTO WELLINGTON

First published 1994

British Library Cataloguing in Publication Data
A catalogue record for this book is available from the British Library

Library of Congress Cataloguing in Publication Data
A catalogue record for this book is available from the Library of Congress

ISBN 0 240 51385 1

Typeset by Tek-Art, Croydon, Surrey
Printed and bound in Great Britain by Clays, St Ives plc

Preface

The technical aspects of photography and imaging cover a wide range of ideas and topics drawn from optics, chemistry, engineering, electronics and visual perception, that bring together the mature technology of silver halide systems in the form of photographic materials with the newer and fast evolving technologies of electronic imaging and digital photography. Common to all such knowledge however are the additional craft skills required to produce a successful image as previsualised, involving or including controlled manipulation of images at the camera, recording and post production stages.

This book, as one of a related series, presents a large amount of detailed data mainly in the form of tables and diagrams on specific topics to supplement the information covering relevant theory, practice and applications that are provided in the other volumes.

To ensure authoritative, contemporary information and details, the material is drawn from several sources, including the Focal Encyclopedia of Photography, third edition, edited by Leslie Stroebel and Richard Zakia, published in 1993. This massive volume has entries compiled by 90 contributors and gives extensive coverage of most aspects of photography, movie production, video, electronic and digital imaging. The selected extracts are largely unaltered but some have been further edited in content to suit the overall subject of the Pocket Book or possibly modified in details to conform to European practices as distinct from those in North America.

Other sources are Applied Photographic Optics, second edition, by Sidney Ray, published in 1994; The Manual of Photography, eighth edition, by Ralph Jacobson, Sidney Ray and Geoffrey Attridge, published in 1988 and The Professional Guide to Photo Data, by Richard Platt, published in 1991.

Coverage includes abbreviations, units, weights and measures, formulae, photographic materials, lens and camera data, lighting and exposure data, printing and processing, publications and miscellaneous topics.

Companion volumes in the Pocket Book series include Photographic Imaging and Electronic Photography, Photographic Chemistry and Processing, Photographic Lenses and Optics, Photographic Printing and Enlarging, Photographic Technology and Image Science.

S F Ray

Contents

1 Abbreviations acronyms and symbols

A Ampere; Angstrom unit; CIE standard illuminant (2855.5 K); Automatic
a Absorption coefficient
A&B Designation of motion-picture film rolls or orientations
AAVT Association of Audio-Visual Technicians
ABC Automatic beam control
AC Alternating current
AC/DC Alternating current/direct current
ACTV Advanced compatible television
ACVL Association of Cinema and Video Laboratories (USA)
AD Analog-to-digital
ADC Analog-to-digital converter
ADP Automatic data processing
ADT Automatic data transmission; Automatic double tracking
AE Automatic exposure
AECT Association for Educational Communications & Technology
AES Audio Engineering Society (USA)
AF Automatic focus; Audio frequency
AFC Automatic frequency control
AFNOR Association Français de Normalisation (France)
AFP Association of Federal Photographers
AFPF Association Française de Production de Films (France)
AFS Aerial film speed
AG All-glass
Ag Silver
AGC Automatic gain control
AgX Silver halide
AHSP Association for High Speed Photography
AIGA America Institute of Graphic Arts
AIIM Association for Information and Image Management
AIPAD Association of International Photography Art Dealers
AL Automatic loading
alpha Absorption factor/ absorptance (Greek letter *a*)
ALU Arithmetic logic unit
AM Amplitude modulation
AMI Amplified MOS intelligent imager
AMII Association for Multi-Image International
amp Ampere
AN Antinewton
ANSI American National Standards Institute

APA	Advertising Photographers of America; Architectural Photographers of America
APAG	American Photographic Artisans Guild
APCL	Association of Professional Color Laboratories (Joined PMA 1989)
APEX	Additive System of Photographic Exposure
API	Associated Photographers International
APIP	Association of Professional Investigative Photographers
APL	Association of Photographic Laboratories
APSA	Associate of the Photographic Society of America
APSE	Abstracts of Photographic Science & Engineering (1962–1972)
AR	Aspect ratio; Analytical reagent
ARPS	Associate of the Royal Photographic Society
ASA	Acoustical Society of America; Formerly, American Standards Association; ANSI filmspeed system
asb	Apostilb
ASC	American Society of Cinematographers
ASCII	American Standard Code for Information Interchange
ASFP	Association of Specialized Film Producers (UK)
ASIFA	Association Internationale du Film d'Animation
ASMP	Society of Photographers in Communications (formerly, American Society of Magazine Photographers)
ASP	American Society of Photogrammetry
ASPP	American Society of Picture Professionals
ASPRS	American Society of Photogrammetry and Remote Sensing
ASTM	American Society for Testing Materials
ATSC	Advanced Television Systems Committee (USA)
auto	Automatic
AV	Audiovisual
A_v	Aperture value (APEX)
AVA	Audio Visual Association (UK)
AVC	Automatic volume control
AVMA	Audio Visual Management Association
AWG	American wire gauge
B	Bulb, shutter speed setting; CIE standard illuminant; Brightness
BABT	British Approvals Board for Telecommunications
BAFTA	British Academy of Film and Television Arts
B-&-W	Black-and-white
BC	Battery capacitor
BCPS	Beam candlepower-second
BCU	Big closeup
BFI	British Film Institute

BISFA	British Industrial and Scientific Film Association
BIPP	British Institute of Professional Photography
bít	Binary digit
BJT	Bipolar junction transistor
BKSTS	British Kinematograph, Sound, and Television Society
BL	Behind lens
Blix	Combination bleach and fix colour processing solution
BOD	Biochemical oxygen demand
bp	Boiling point
BP	Back projection
B/P	Blueprint
BPA	Biological Photographic Association
BPMA	British Photographic Manufacturers Association
BPS	British Photogrammetry Society; Bits per second
BS	British Standard
BSI	British Standards Institution
BTL	Behind-the-lens
B_v	Light value (APEX)
B-W	Black-and-white
C	Capacitance
C	Celcius (Centigrade); Chrominance; CIE standard illuminant; Colour; Coulomb; C-mount
c	Candela (also cd); Velocity of light in a vacuum
©	Copyright
CAD	Computer-aided design
CAM	Computer-aided manufacture
CAR	Computer-aided retrieval
CAT	Computerized axial tomography
CAV	Constant angular velocity
CC	Colour compensating (filter)
cc	Cubic centimeter (also cu cm)
CCD	Charge-coupled device
CCR	Camera cassette recorder
CCIR	Comite Consultatif International de Radio (International Radio Consultative Committee)
CC	Camera control unit
cd	Candela (also c)
CD	Compact disc
CD-I	Compact disc interactive
CD-ROM	Compact disc-read-only memory
CD-V	Compact disc-video
CdS	Cadmium sulphide (photocell)
CD-WORM	Compact disc-write once/read many
CEI	Comite European d'Imprimerie (European printing standards organization)
cell	Cellulose acetate sheet
CEPS	Colour electronic prepress system

CFF	Critical fusion frequency; Critical flicker frequency
CG	Character generator
CGI	Computer graphics interactive; Computer graphics imaging
CGM	Computer graphics metafile
cgs	Centimeter-gram-second system
CI	Contrast index
CID	Charge-injection device
CIE	Commission Internationale de l'Eclairage (International Commission on Illumination)
cine	Cinematography
CIR	Colour infrared
C-line	Radiation having a wavelength of 656.3 nm
CLUT	Colour look-up table
CLV	Constant linear velocity
cm	Centimeter
C-mount	Lens mount
CMYK	Cyan, magenta, yellow, and black
COD	Chemical oxygen demand
CODEC	Coder/decoder
COM	Computer output microfilm
COMMAG	Composite magnetic
COMOPT	Composite optical
cos	Cosine
CP	Candlepower
CPD	Charge-priming device
CPU	Central processing unit
CRA	Camera-ready artwork
CRI	Colour-rendering index
CRT	Cathode-ray tube
C/S	Cycles per second
CSBTS	China State Bureau of Technical Supervision
CSN	Federal Office for Standards and Measurement (Czechoslovakia)
CT	Continuous tone; Colour temperature
CTF	Contrast transfer function
CU	Closeup
cu	Cubic
CYSI/CYG	The colour you see is the colour you get
D	Density
D-1, D-2, D-3, D-5	Video formats
DA	Digital-to-analog
DAC	Digital-to-analog converter
DAD	Digital audio disc
DAT	Digital audio tape
dB	Decibel
DC	Direct current
DCS	Digital camera system
DCT	Discrete cosine transform (compression algorithm)
DDES	Digital data exchange standard
DGPh	Deutsch Gesellschaft fur Photographie

	(Germany)
DIC	Differential interference contrast
DIN	Deutsche Industrie Norm (Germany)
DIP	Dual in-line package
DIR	Development-inhibitor-release
DL	Difference limen (Also JND, just-noticeable difference)
D-line	Radiation having a wavelength of 589.6 nm
D-log H	Density-logarithm exposure
DM&E	Dialog, music, and effects
Dmax	Maximum density
Dmin	Minimum density
DN	Digital number
DNA	Deutschen Normenausschuss (German standards organization)
DOF	Depth of field
DOP	Developing-out paper
DOS	Disk operating system
DP	Director of photography
DPCM	Differential pulse code modulation
DPI	Dots per inch
DPM	Dots per millimetre
Dr	Reflection density
DRAM	Dynamic random access memory
DRAW	Direct read after write
DSP	Digital signal processing
DSU	Digital storage unit
Dr	Transmission density
DTC	Dual time code
DTP	Desktop publishing
DTR	Diffusion transfer reversal
DTV	Desktop video
D2T2	Dye diffusion thermal transfer
DU	Dual (magnetic sound tracks)
dupe	Duplicate
DVI	Digital video interactive
DVR	Digital video recording
DW	Double weight
DX	Photographic bar code; Double exposure
aE	Illuminance/irradiance (international standard); Exposure (nonstandard)
e	Radiant energy; Base of natural logarithms
EAVA	European Audio-Visual Association
EBR	Electron beam recording
EBU	European Broadcasting Unit
ECPS	Effective candle power seconds
ECU	Extreme closeup
EE	Electric eye
EEPROM	Electronically erasable programmable read only memory
EFX	Effects (motion-picture code)
EI	Exposure index
EIA	Electronics Industry Association
EM	Electron microscope

EMF	Electromotive force
EMR	Electromagnetic radiation
EMU	Electromagnetic unit
END	Equivalent neutral density
ENG	Electronic news gathering
EO	Emulsion out
EO	Electro-optics
EPIC	Evidence Photographers International Council
EQE	Equivalent quantum efficiency
EROS	Earth resources observations systems
ERTS	Earth resources technology satellite
ESCSC	Electronic Still Camera Standardization Committee
ESU	Electrostatic unit
$\mathbf{E_v}$	Exposure value (APEX) (Also EV)
eV	Electron volt
EVGA	Extended video graphic array
EVOP	Evolutionary operations
EVR	Electronic video recording
EXP	Exposed
F	Fahrenheit; Farad; Fast (type of flashbulbs)
f	Focal length
***f*-**	f-number (word)
***f*/**	f-number (number, such as *f*/16)
FAP	Front axial projection
fax	Facsimile
fc	Footcandle
FET	Field effect transistor
FF	Flare factor
FI	Fade in
FIAF	Federation Internationale des Archives du Film
FIAP	Federation Internationale de l'Art Photographique
FKGT	Fernseh-und Kinotechnischen Gesellschaft (German film and television technical society)
fL	Footlambert (luminance)
F-line	Radiation having a wavelength of 486.1 nm
fl oz	Fluid ounce
FM	Frequency modulation
FO	Fade out
FOP	Friends of Photography
FOV	Field of view
FP	Focal plane; Front projection
FPE	Fellowship of Photographic Educators
fpm	Feet per minute; Frames per minute
fps	Feet per second; Foot-pound-second; Frames per second
FPSA	Fellowship of the Photographic Society of America
FRPS	Fellow of the Royal Photographic Society of Great Britain
FSAP	Farm Security Administration Photography
***f*/64**	*f*/64 Group
ft	Foot

FX	Effects (motion picture)
G	Gradient; Selwyn granularity; Gauss
$\overline{\mathbf{G}}$	G bar, average gradient
g	Gram (also gm)
gal	Gallon
GATF	Graphic Arts Technical Foundation
gel	Gelatin
GFCI	Ground fault circuit interrupter
GG	Ground glass
GHz	Gigahertz (one billion cycles per second)
gm	Gram
GN	Guide number
***G*-N**	*G*-Number, or photometric aperture
GOST	Gosudarstvenny Obshchesoyuzny Standart (USSR, now CIS, standards organization)
gr	Grain
GRIN	Graded refractive index
GUI	Graphical users interface
G/V	General view
H	Photographic exposure (international); Hue (Munsell); Henry (inductance)
H&D	Hurter and Driffield
HARP	High-gain, avalanche-rushing amorphous photoconductor
HD	High density
HDTV	High-definition television
HE	Head end (motion picture)
HI	High intensity (arc lamp)
HICON	High contrast
HID	High-intensity discharge
HI8	Video format
HIRF	High-irradiance reciprocity failure
HI VF	(High-band still video)
HMI	H (Hg/mercury), M (medium arc), I (iodide) — (metal halide lamp)
HP	High pressure (mercury vapour lamp)
HR	High resolution
HSSV	High-speed shuttered video
Hz	Hertz, or cycles per second
I	Electrical current; Radiant intensity (I_e) or luminous intensity (I_v); Instantaneous (shutter speed); (formerly Illuminance)
IBN	Institute Belge de Normalisation (Belgium standards institute)
IC	Integrated circuit
ICHSPP	International Congress on High-Speed Photography & Photonics
ICI	International Commission of Illumination
ICIA	International Communications Industries Association
ICO	International Commission for Optics
ICP	International Center of Photography

ICR	International Council for Reprography
IDF	Intermediate donor film
IEC	International Electrotechnical Commission
IEEE	Institute of Electrical & Electronic Engineers
IFPA	International Fire Photographers Association
IIP	Institute of Incorporated Photographers
IIPC	India International Photographic Council
IMBI	Institute of Medical and Biological Illustration
IMC	Image-motion compensation
IMLA	International Minilab Association
IMPA	International Museum Photographers Association
IMP/GEH	International Museum of Photography/George Eastman House
inf	Infinity
I/O	Input/output
IPC	International Photographic Council
IPI	Image Permanence Institute
IPOSA	International Photo Optical Show Association
ips	Inches per second
IR	Infra-red
IRE	(Formerly) Institute of Radio Engineers, (now) a measurement unit
IS&T	Society for Imaging Science and Technology/SPSE
ISCC	Intersociety Colour Council
ISDN	Integrated Services Digital Network
ISO	International Organization for Standardization (International Standards Organization)
ISP	International Society for Photogrammetry
ITVA	International Television Association
IU	International unit
IVLA	International Visual Literacy Association
J	Joule
JISC	Japanese Industrial Standards Committee
JND	Just-noticeable difference
JPEG	Joint Photo Experts Group
K	Kelvin
k	Kilo
Kb	Kilobit
kB	Kilobyte
kg	Kilogram
kHz	Kilohertz
kW	Kilowatt
L	Inductance; Luminance (L_v) or Radiance (L_e); Lambert; Long-exposure colour film
l	litre(s)
lab	Laboratory
LATD	Large area transmission density
lb	Pound
LCD	Liquid crystal display
LCL	Lower control limit

LCLV	Liquid crystal light value
LE	Life expectancy
LED	Light emitting diode
LIRF	Low-irradiancc reciprocity failure
lith	Lithographic
LLL	Low light level
lm	Lumen
l/mm	Lines per millimeter
lm-s	Lumen-second
ln	Natural logarithm
log	Logarithm
lpi	Lines per inch
lpm	Lines pairs per millimeter
LS	Long shot; Loudspeaker
LSF	Line spread function
LUT	Look-up table
Lvr	Longitudinal video recording
LW	Line work (file)
lx	Lux (meter-candle)
lx-sec	lux-second (meter-candle-second)
M	Magnification (Also R, reproduction ratio); Medium (speed flashbulbs); Radiant exitance (M_e) or luminous exitance (M_v); Exitance; Mega- (1,000,000)
m	Meter; Milli- (1/1000th)
mag	Magnetic
MAGB	Microfilm Association of Great Britain
M&E	Music and effect track
mat	Matrix
Mavica	Magnetic Video Camera (Trademark)
Mb	Megabit
MB	Megabyte
MBPS	Megabytes per second/megabits per second
mc	meter-candle
mcs	meter-candle-second
MCU	Medium closeup
mg	Milligram
MHCP	Mean horizontal candlepower
MHz	Megahertz
mike	Microphone
mil	One-thousandth of an inch
milli-	One-thousandth
min	Minute
MIPS	Million instructions per second
mired	Micro-reciprocal-degree
mks	Meter, kilogram, second
mL	Millilambert
ml	Millilitre
MLS	Medium long shot
mm	Millimetre
MOD	Minimum operating distance
MOS	Mit out sound; Metal-oxide semiconductor
MPAA	Motion Picture Association of America
MPC	Multimedia personal computer

MPCD	Minimum perceptible colour difference
MPDFA	Master Photo Dealers and Finishers Association
MPEG	Motion Picture Experts Group
MQ	Metol-hydroquinone (developer)
MRI	Magnetic resonance imaging
MS	Medium shot
ms	Millisecond (1/1000th)
MSCP	Mean spherical candlepower
MSDS	Material safety data sheet
MTF	Modulation transfer function
MUM	Maximum useful magnification
n	Nano (1/1,000,000,000th)
n	Index of refraction
NA	Numerical aperture
NAB	National Association of Broadcasters
NAF	Numerical aperture of fibre optics bundle
NAPET	National Association of Photo Equipment Technicians
NAPhA	North American Photonics Association
NAPM	National Association of Photographic Manufacturers
NAPP	National Aerial Photography Program
NBS	National Bureau of Standards
NC	Nocurl coating
NCS	Natural colour system
ND	Neutral density
NEP	Noise-equivalent power
NFS	Not for sale
NG	No good
NHAP	National High Altitude Photography
nicad	Nickel-cadmium cell
nm	Nanometer
NPIA	National Photographic Instructors Association
NPN	One of two types of bipolar junction transistors
NPPA	National Press Photographers Association
ns	Nanosecond
NSA	National Stereoscopic Association
NTSC	National Television Standards Committee
nu(ν)-number	Index of refraction (Greek letter) (Syn.: v-*number*)
O	Opacity
OCR	Optical character reader/recognition
ON	Original negative
op	Optical (op art)
OPT FX	Optical effects
ortho	Orthochromatic
OS	Operating system
OTF	Optical transfer function; Off the film
oz	Ounce
P	Power (radiant flux other than light); Power (electrical)

p	*para* (organic chemistry)
PA	Public address
PACA	Picture Agency Council of America
pAg	Silver ion concentration
PAI	Photographic Administrators, Inc.
PAL	Phase alternative line, European colour television coding system
pan	Panchromatic
PASF	Photographic Art and Science Foundation
PC	Personal computer; Pin-cylinder (connector); Phase change (disk); Plastic-coated
PCB	Printed circuit board
PCM	Pulse code modulation
PCMI	Photochromic microimage process
PD	Physical development; Potential difference
PE	Polyester; Photoelectric (cell)
Pe	Excitation purity (colorimetry)
PEC	Photoelectric cell
PEP	Photoelectrophoresis
PF	Power factor
pH	Hydrogen ion concentration
phi(ø)	Radiant flux or luminous flux (Greek letter)
photo	Photograph; Photography
PHS	Photographic Historical Society
PIC	Photographic Industry Council
pico	10^{-12}
PIP	Persistent internal polarization
pix	Picture (slang)
pixel	Picture element
PL	Photo League
PMA	Photographic Manufacturers Association
PMAI	Photo Marketing Association International
PMDA	Photographic Manufacturers and Distributors Association
PMS	Pantone matching system
PMT	Photomultiplier tube
PNP	One of two types of bipolar junction transistors
POP	Printing-out paper
POTA	Photo Optics Technical Area (POTA developer)
POV	Point of view
PPA	Pictorial Photographers of America
PPM	Pulses per minute
PPofA	Professional Photographers of America
pps	Pictures per second
PQ	Phenidone-hydroquinone (developer)
pro	Professional
ps	Picosecond (10^{-12} second)
PSA	Photographic Society of America
PSC	Portable single camera
PSF	Point spread function
PSPA	Professional School Photographers Association
pt	Pint
PTF	Phase transfer function
PV	Panchromatic viewing (filter)

PVC	Polyvinyl chloride
PWP	Professional Women Photographers
Q	Quantity of energy (Q_e) or light (Q_v); Quality (electrical circuits); Q-factor (Callier coefficient); Q-switch (lasers)
QA	Quality assurance
QC	Quality control
QI	Quartz-iodine (lamp)
qt	Quart
Q-FACTOR	See *Callier coefficient.*
R	Reproduction ratio/Scale of reproduction (Also magnification); Resistance; Roentgen
rad	Radian (unit of absorbed radiation)
RAM	Random access memory
R&D	Research and development
RAR	Rapid access recording
RAT	Reflected, absorbed, transmitted
RC	Resin coated
RD	Reconstructed distribution (colorimetry)
rep	Representative
RF	Roll film; Rangefinder; Radio frequency; Reciprocity failure
RGB	Red, green, blue (video)
RH	Relative humidity
RIAA	Recording Industries Association of America
RIFF	Raster image file format
RIP	Raster image processor
RISC	Reduced instruction set
RLF	Reciprocity law failure
RMS	Root mean square
ROM	Read-only memory
ROP	Run of press
RP	Resolving power
rpm	Revolutions per minute
rps	Revolutions per second
RPSGB	Royal Photographic Society of Great Britain
RTA	Real time analyzer
RTS	Royal Television Society
S	Short (exposure colour film); Slow (type of flashbulb); CIE standard illuminants (Subscripts A, B, C, E)
s	second (also sec)
SA	Spherical aberration
SBC	Silicon blue cell
SCR	Silicon controlled rectifier
SCSI	Small computer systems interface
SDT	Silver diffusion transfer
sec	Second
SECAM	Sequential Couleur A Mémoire (French television system)
SED	Spectral energy distribution
SEM	Scanning electron microscope

SEPMAG	Separate Magnetic (sound track)
SF	Sheet film
SFPC	Société Francais de Photographie et de Cinematography
SFX	Sound effects
SGO	Second generation original
SHSV	Shuttered high speed video
SI	Systéme International d'Unités (System of international units of measurement)
SIC	Semiconductor integrated circuit
SLR	Single-lens reflex (camera); Subject luminance range
SM	Speed midget (flashlamp)
SMPTE	Society of Motion Picture and Television Engineers
SMT	System modulation transfer (acutance)
S/N	Signal-to-noise ratio
SNR	Signal-to-noise ratio
SOP	Standard operating procedure
SPC	Society of Photographers in Communications
SPC	Society of Photographic Counsellors
SPE	Society for Photographic Education
SPFE	Society of Photo-Finishing Engineers
SPG	Sync-pulse generator
sp gr	Specific gravity
SPIE	Society of Photo-optical Instrumentation Engineers
SPL	Sound pressure level
SPSE	See Society for Imaging Science and Technology, IS&T
SPT	Society of Photo-technologists
SPV	Society of Professional Videographers
SR	Society of Radiographers
sr	Steradian
SRAM	Static random access memory
SS	Stainless steel
S/S	Same size
SSA	Studio Suppliers Association
SSR	Solid-state relay
SSVR	Solid state video recorder
STC	Single time code
STPP	Society of Teachers of Professional Photography
S_V	Speed value (APEX)
SV	Still video
SVA	Stereo variable area
S-VHS	Super-VHS
SW	Single weight
sync	Synchronized, synchronization
T	Time (shutter setting); Transmittance; Tesla
t	Time (as in $H = E \times t$); Temperature
T-	*T*-number (word); T-stop
T/	*T*-number (number, such as T/8)
TAGA	Technical Association for the Graphic Arts

TCIP	Time code in picture
TE	Tail end (motion-picture film)
tele	Telephoto
TEM	Transmission electron microscope
3D	Three-dimensional
TL	Through-the-lens (also TTL)
TLR	Twin-lens reflex (camera)
TMD	Thermal magnetic duplication
TMO	Thermal magneto optical (disc)
TOC	Target object contrast
TTL	Through-the-lens (also TL)
TTL-OTF	Through-the-lens off the film
TTS	True to scale
$\mathbf{T}_{v}$	Time value (APEX)
TV	Television
TVR	Television recording (See kinescope)
TX	Transmission
u	Object distance
UCA	Undercolour addition
UCL	Upper control limit
UCR	Undercolour removal
UCS	Uniform chromaticity scale; Uniform colour space
UHF	Ultra-high frequency
UNI	Ente Nazional Italiano di Unificaszione (Italian standards organization)
UPAA	University Photographers Association of America
US	Uniform system (Obsolete aperture calibration)
USP	United States Pharmacopeia
UV	Ultraviolet
UVA	Ultraviolet (long wavelength)
UVB	Ultraviolet (short wavelength)
V	Volt
v	value (APEX system); image distance (Optics); velocity
***ν*-number**	Index of refraction (Syn.: Nu-number, Abbe number)
VA	Variable area (soundtrack)
VBI	Vertical blanking interval
VCNA	Video colour negative analyzer
VCR	Videocassette recorder
VD	Variable density (soundtrack)
VDT	Video display terminal; Visual display terminal
VDU	Video display unit; Visual display unit
VFS	Video floppy system
VGA	Video graphics array
VHF	Very high frequency
VHS	Video Home System (Trade name)
VHS-C	VHS-Compact
VIBGYOR	Violet, indigo, blue, green, yellow, orange, red
VITC	Vertical interval time code
VLF	Very low frequency

VLP	Very long play
VLS	Very long shot
VO	Voice over (motion pictures)
VOM	Volt-ohm meter
VT	Videotape
VTR	Videotape recorder
VU	Volume unit
W	Watt
WA	Wide angle
WB	White balance
WFM	Wave form monitor
WHNPA	White House News Photographers Association
WORM	Write once/read many
WPI	Wedding Photographers International
X	Electronic-flash synchronization (X-sync); Degree of enlargement (4X)
X	Coordinate (Abscissa)
x-	x-ray
XA	Extended architecture (computers)
XCU	Extreme closeup
Y	Coordinate (ordinate); Luminance
YC	Luminance, chrominance
YCC	Luminance, chrominance, chrominance
yd	Yard
YIQ	Luminance and two colour-difference signals
YUV	Luminance and two colour-difference signals
Z	Coordinate in XYZ systems; Impedence

Greek Alphabet and Letter Symbols

Name	Caps	L.c.	Used for
Alpha	A		
		α	Light *absorption factor;* absorptance.
Beta	B		
		β	*Luminance factor.*
Gamma	Γ		Gamma function.
		γ	Slope of straight line portion of *D-Log H curve; γ bar gamma (Average gradient).*
Delta	Δ		Change in a variable (e.g. ΔD, ΔLog H).
		δ	Density (mass of unit volume of a substance).
Epsilon	E		
		ϵ	*Emissivity.*
Zeta	Z		
		ζ	
Eta	H		
		η	*Luminous efficiency* of a source; *Lumens* per *watt.*

Theta	Θ		
		θ	Angle.
Iota	Ι		
		ι	
Kappa	Κ		
		κ	Electrolytic conductivity.
Lambda	Λ		
		λ	*Wave length* (λ_d dominant, λ_o complementary wave length).
Mu	Μ		Magnetic flux.
		μ	*Refractive index; Micron;* micro (10^{-6}); μμ micro-micro.
Nu	Ν		
		ν	Constringence (*Abbe number*); *Frequency* of EMR velocity; ν *Wave number.*
Xi	Ξ		
		ξ	
Omicron	Ο		
		ο	
Pi	Π		
		π	Ratio of circumference to diameter of a circle 3.14159.
Rho	Ρ		
		ρ	Light reflection factor (*reflectance*); Density (in mechanics).
Sigma	Σ		Sum of.
		σ	*Granularity;* conductivity; *Poisson* ratio; *Standard deviation*; Electric charge density; *Stefan-Boltzmann constant.*
Tau	Τ		
		τ	Transmission factor (*transmittance*).
Upsilon	Υ		
		υ	
Phi	Φ		*Luminous flux*; Magnetic flux; Φe radiant flux
		φ	*Phase* displacement.
Chi	Χ		–
		χ	
Psi	Ψ		Electric flux.
		ψ	Angle.
Omega	Ω		Solid angle; Ohm; mΩ megohm.
		ω	*Frequency*; Angular velocity; *Solid angle*; Dispersive power.

2 Photographic chronologies

2.1 PHOTOGRAPHIC PROCESSES: An outline history

Classification of photographic processes may be made according to the chemical components and their functions, the method of obtaining a final copy, or the intended application.

Since 1800, salts of silver formed with members of the halogen family, chlorine, bromine, and iodine, have constituted the basis of most photochemical imaging. Exposure causes these salts to form a latent image that can be developed out or, with sufficient exposure, printed out. Fixing in sodium thiosulphate or ammonium thiosulphate removes unexposed and undeveloped salts, rendering the image safe in light. Silver halides are used in most colour imaging as well; they are used to form the image and are removed after dye formation in chromogenic processes, or after dye destruction in dye-bleach processes.

Some iron salts are also sensitive to light. The reduction of iron from its ferric (3+) to its ferrous (2+) state is the basis of the chrysotype, cyanotype, kallitype, platinotype, and Vandyke processes. The ferro-cupric and ferro-gallic high contrast processes are also iron-based.

When a colloid such as gelatin, casein, albumen, shellac, or gum arabic is sensitized with potassium, sodium, or ammonium bichromate, the emulsion changes upon exposure to light. The colloid may become insoluble if previously soluble; it may no longer absorb water and swell up, or it may lose its surface tackiness. For example, powder processes are based on loss of tackiness, creating ceramic and photomechanical applications. The carbon, carbro, gum bichromate, bromide and dye transfer processes also employ bichromates, as do some silkscreening techniques.

Diazo copying processes employ diazonium salts that are destroyed when they are exposed by ultraviolet, violet, or blue light. The salts can couple with aniline to form coloured compounds.

Another way of classifying photographic processes is according to the way they arrive at a final product. Of the three viable photographic systems published in 1839, W. H. Fox Talbot's was a negative-positive process, and L. J. M. Daguerre and Hyppolyte Bayard made direct positives. Reversal processing was first achieved by C. Russell in 1862. Transfer of a chemical image, a physical image or an emulsion from one support to another is the basis of dye transfer, carbro, bromoil, and diffusion transfer processes.

Colour processes may be additive, combining red, green, and blue elements, or subtractive, combining yellow, magenta, and cyan. Some record images on panchromatic black-and-white emulsions by employing linear or lenticular screens to separate white light into its primary components. Some colour processes, such as tri-colour carbro and dye transfer, rely on the assembly of a colour image from separate matrices.

Development of an image may be physical or chemical. In physical development, the silver forming the image is supplied by the developer rather than by the emulsion, essentially silver plating the latent image specks. In chemical development, the developer reduces exposed silver halides to form metallic silver and halogen ions. Tanning developers that harden the gelatin of the emulsion must first operate chemically; it is the developer oxidation products that harden the gelatin.

Photomechanical reproduction is a distinct branch of photography that employs many of the processes described in conjunction with general purpose photography.

Letterpress line blocks are made by making a negative on lithographic film from a line drawing and exposing it by contact onto a zinc plate with a dichromated albumen coating after which the plate is etched.

Halftone blocks begin with a litho film negative made through a halftone screen. The negative is contact printed on a zinc or copper plate coated with a light-sensitive fish glue ammonium dichromate solution; the plate is then etched.

Offset lithography also uses halftone images produced from continuous tone images by means of a halftone screen, and a plate coated with dichromated colloid, but here the hardened colloid may be used directly for printing.

Photogravure etches the image into a printing cylinder. Carbon tissue bathed in potassium dichromate is exposed through a photogravure screen and transferred to a copper cylinder where the soluble, unexposed gelatin is washed away. The tissue forms a resist that determines where the cylinder will be etched with ferric chloride.

Colour printing processes use photographically made separations to prepare plates that print yellow, magenta, cyan, and sometimes black. Specialized presses can print six or more impressions in one pass through the press, and offer the option of finish coatings over colour.

COLOUR PROCESSES

Chromogenic Development Today, most negative and reversal colour photochemical imaging systems employ chromogenic development to form dye images. The technology has its roots in the textile industry of the nineteenth century in which dye-coupling was used to form colours in the fibres of fabrics. In 1873, H. W. Vogel used dyes to extend the spectral response of silver halides, making orthochromatic collodion plates. Research by R. E. Liesegang, H. Luppo-Cramer, B. Homolka and others into dye characteristics, oxidation, and development enabled R. Fischer and H. Siegrist to patent a practical system of chromogenic development in 1912.

Negative films with conventional integral tripack emulsions form silver and dye images during the single development step. Reduction of the silver image from silver halides produces oxidation products that then react with dye couplers in each emulsion layer to form subtractive dyes. To keep the couplers from migrating into other layers, forming inappropriate colours, they may be encapsulated in shells of colloids that are permeable but not soluble in the processing solution, or they may be anchored in place by attaching them to long, inert hydrocarbon chains that make the couplers too heavy to move or too large to slip through gelatin. Yellow dye is formed in the blue-sensitive layer; magenta dye is formed in the green-sensitive layer, and cyan dye is formed in the red-sensitive layer.

Colour negatives have a characteristic orange cast, which is a mask that compensates for unwanted absorptions by the cyan and magenta dye layers. One method of generating the mask incorporates yellow couplers in the magenta layer, and orange or red couplers in the cyan layer. Oxidation products form dyes that are visible in the unexposed areas of the negative.

Because developer oxidation products join with colour formers to produce dye, customary antioxidants such as sodium sulphite would inhibit dye formation. Antioxidant concentrations are necessarily kept very low, with the consequence that colour developers have very short working lives.

Bleaching and fixing remove the silver image, leaving the dye. The bleach is a complex mixture that forms silver bromide from the silver in the image, enabling an ammonium thiosulphate-based fixer to complete the task of silver removal. The bleach and fixer are often combined in one step, called blix. After washing, a stabilizer with little or no formaldehyde is used to preserve the dyes.

Chromogenic integral tripack colour reversal materials are similar in many respects to their negative counterparts. A latent image is first formed in silver halides, but the first development is black and white only, forming a silver negative image. The remaining unexposed or undeveloped areas of the emulsion are then either re-exposed to light or sensitized in a fogging bath, forming a positive latent image. The second development works like the developer in negative processing. Colour couplers in each emulsion layer react with oxidation products in the developer, forming subtractive dyes, as well as a positive silver image. Bleach then converts the silver of both images to soluble compounds that are removed by the fixer. Washing and stabilization follow.

Prints can be made chromogenically from either negatives or positives. Negatives are printed on integral tripack papers and display materials that are like negatives without the compensation mask. Development follows the same steps.

Positives are printed on integral tripack materials that mirror positives, requiring re-exposure to light or a reversal bath.

Modern formulations of processing solutions are made with concern for safety and environmental considerations. Because photochemical systems are in use throughout the world, manufacturers must maintain compliance with a maze of often-contradictory regulations. There is also a need to avoid infringing on industrial patents, necessitating the search for new ways to perform old tasks.

Differential Dye Diffusion Kodachrome was invented in the 1930s by Mannes, Godowsky, and a research team at Eastman Kodak. They solved the problem of making the dyes stay in their respective emulsion layers by adding the dyes during processing. The film has three silver halide emulsion layers without colour couplers. In a highly sophisticated processor, the antihalation backing is removed; silver negative images are developed; the film is exposed to red light through the back and developed with cyan-forming developer yielding a cyan and silver positive; the film is exposed to blue light from the top and developed in yellow forming developer, yielding a yellow and silver positive; a fogging developer forms a positive magenta dye and silver image. Bleach then converts all the silver to soluble compounds that are removed by fixer, leaving a dye image.

The skilled personnel required for the performance of these tasks, the expense and relative scarcity of the equipment involved, and the dramatic improvements in chromogenically processed reversal materials that can be processed quickly and successfully almost anywhere all call the long-term future of Kodachrome process materials into question.

Dye Diffusion Transfer The formation of colour images by means of the diffusion transfer process is, currently, the sole province of Polaroid. In the 1980s, Agfa marketed a dye-diffusion-transfer integral-colour printing material called Agfachrome Speed, and Kodak offered a line of peel-apart printing materials called Ektaflex, as well as instant colour print films. Now, Polaroid has peel-apart and integral diffusion transfer materials. They have red, green, and blue sensitive layers interleaved with metallized dye developers that form cyan, magenta, and yellow dyes. The material is exposed and passed through rollers that break the pods containing separate processing solutions for each emulsion layer. The developed dye/developer molecules are immobilized while the undeveloped molecules can migrate through the emulsion to the mordanted receiver where the positive dye image is formed.

Peel-apart materials protect the light-sensitive components until processing is complete, and facilitate the disposal of all substances consumed and no longer necessary. Integral materials enjoy no such luxuries. They protect the emulsion after exposure by generating an opacifying layer that reverses itself at the conclusion of processing. They form a pigment barrier layer between the image and the negative to conceal and isolate processing byproducts and provide a background for viewing.

Screen Processes Before effective chromogenic materials were available, systems by Joly, the Lumière Brothers, Dufay, and Finlay, as well as Kodak and Agfa, all used screens to divide light into its primary components. Some screens were lenticular, some were coloured lines, and some were mosaic or reseau. All split the light on its way to a panchromatic black-and-white emulsion, usually reversal processed. While the details varied, most used white light projected through the back to modulate the intensity of the light reaching the screen. As the light passed through, a colour image was constructed. Currently, Polaroid Polachrome 35mm film employs a screen in conjunction with a peel-apart diffusion transfer emulsion to produce an additive three colour positive image.

Dye Transfer The dye transfer process is an assembly process for making colour prints from colour positives or negatives. Two kinds of matrix film are used – orthochromatic and panchromatic. The panchromatic film is used when separations are to be made directly from colour negatives or internegatives onto the matrix film, eliminating the need to make separation negatives. However, significant control over the final image can be exercised while making separation negatives.

In either case, the separations are made in registration through red, green, and blue filters, eventually producing the matrices that will print cyan, magenta, and yellow dyes. The matrix film is exposed through the back because its dichromated gelatin emulsion is subject to hardening in a tanning developer where the emulsion has been exposed. The unexposed and unhardened parts of the emulsion are on the top and can then be washed away in warm water, leaving a relief image in gelatin.

The matrices are soaked in their respective dyes and applied to the print, cyan first, then magenta and yellow, in register. Multiple applications, changes in soaking and rinsing procedures, and modifications of the dye baths all provide additional controls. The intricacy of the process is a function of the degree of control it offers to the skilled practitioner. The dye transfer process is generally regarded as the foremost system of colour printing because of that control, the durability of the prints and the subtlety of the dyes that form the image.

Silver-Dye-Bleach Process The silver-dye-bleach process is an integral tripack system with yellow, magenta, and cyan azo dyes incorporated into the blue-green-, and red sensitive emulsion layers, respectively, during manufacture. After exposure from a colour positive, the material is processed in black-and-white developer to produce a silver image. A strongly acidic dye bleach with an added accelerator causes the destruction of the dyes adjacent to the silver image grains in proportion to the amount of silver bleached. Fixer removes the bleached negative silver image and the unexposed, undeveloped silver halide components of the positive image. The stable, luminous azo dyes that remain correspond to the original positive image.

HISTORY OF PHOTOGRAPHIC PROCESSES

Before the nineteenth century, photography existed as a phantom. Its components had been known for hundreds of years. The Greeks and Egyptians knew substances whose nature was altered by exposure to sunlight. Renaissance painters knew how to project an image onto canvas in a darkened chamber. The growing middle class wanted images of their travels and of family members, and there were scientific and industrial applications waiting eagerly for someone to figure out how to write with light.

Experimentation, discovery, and development in photographic processes in the nineteenth century were concerned first with finding workable materials that would record an image in a reasonable time. Early in the century, exposures lasted 8 hours. Before the end of the century, birds' wings and horses' hooves could be frozen in mid-action.

The impermanence of their work plagued early experimenters. In 1800, Wedgwood and Davy could not prevent their photograms from turning black in light, and the salt used by Talbot and Daguerre in the 1830s was of limited effectiveness. The "hyposulphite of soda" method for making silver halide images permanent was discovered by Sir John Herschel in 1819 and shared generally in 1839. Washing of film and paper were reasonably well understood by the turn of the century.

For daguerreotypists and ferrotypists, the lack of a sufficiently clear base on which to coat emulsions was of little concern; their work couldn't be duplicated anyway. For those who employed negative-positive processes to get multiple prints from individual negatives, paper negatives lacked sufficient translucency for successful printing, even if the paper was waxed. Glass was the next solution, and it was an admirable one except for its weight, fragility, and rigidity. By the end of the century, celluloid roll films could be loaded in daylight.

Early in the century, photographic emulsions had no shelf life at all; they were exposed wet shortly after sensitization, and their effective speed varied with a multitude of factors. Dry plates, sheet film, and roll film were manufactured to standardized sensitometric standards by century's end.

Blue skies and red clothing rendered respectively as white and black were artifacts of silver halide emulsions that were most sensitive at the blue-violet end of the spectrum and saw nothing of the red end. Vogel's discovery of dye-sensitization in 1873 laid the groundwork for orthochromatic and then panchromatic light-sensitive materials, as well as the attainment of the great goal—workable colour photographic systems.

In sum, one might argue that the thrust of photography in the nineteenth century was democratization. It started in the labs of scientists, inventors, and tinkerers, and was sold prepackaged on street corners by the end of the century. The huge—and growing—market for photographic materials provided the profits to fuel the research projects of the twentieth century that gave us faster and more universal processing, dramatically increased film speed, reduced grain size, provided more accurate and more saturated colour, increased convenience in packaging and one-step materials, and a vast range of specialized products for medical, scientific, business, industrial, and military applications.

At the close of the twentieth century, the two principal thrusts in photographic processes are, first, reduced toxicity of the chemicals used in processing and reduced discharge of all contaminants that are produced by photographic processes, and second, a steady movement toward electronics and microprocessors in the management of photographic imaging and processing equipment, and in the acquisition, storage, and manipulation of the images themselves.

Despite the extraordinary quality of current photochemical imaging systems, their continued success depends upon the development of processes that work successfully within the confines of environmental protection. Digital imaging needs to solve storage, cost, and resolution problems, but the market is in place.

The rate of transition from photochemical to digital imaging is what remains to be determined.

PHOTOGRAPHIC PROCESSES: OUTLINE HISTORY

1727 J. H. Schulze, sensitivity to light of silver nitrate with chalk

1772 J. Priestley, *History and Present State of Discoveries Relating to Visions Light and Colours*

1777 C. W. Scheele, silver reduced by light from silver chloride; silver chloride more sensitive to some colours of light (violet, blue) than others; ammonia destroys light sensitivity of silver chloride

1800 Sir W. Herschel, discovery of infra-red

1800 T. Wedgwood and H. Davy, unfixed silver nitrate and silver chloride photograms

1819 Sir J. F. W. Herschel, discovery of thiosulphates and the solution of silver halides by "hypo"

1826 J. N. Niépce, Heliography, exposed areas of bitumen of asphalt became insoluble in lavender oil, a photopolymerization process

1835 W. H. F Talbot, photogenic drawing, printing-out negative and paper sensitized with salt and silver nitrate photopoly merization

1839 L. J. M. Daguerre, daguerreotype process published

1839 H. Bayard, direct-positive paper process

1840 W. H. F. Talbot, calotype, developed-out negative, printed-out positive

1840 N. de St. Victor and R. Hunt, thermography

1842 Sir J. F. W. Herschel, cyanotype, ferroprussiate paper

1844 R. Hunt, ferrous oxalate process, ferrous sulphate development

1847 N. de St. Victor, albumen glass plates

1850 D. Blanquart-Evrard, albumen paper

1851 G. Le Gray, waxed-paper process

1851 F. S. Archer, collodion binder, wet-collodion process

1851 Regnault and Liebig, independently, pyrogallol developer

1852 W. H. F Talbot, photoglyphic engraving

1853 A. A. Martin, tintype, ferrotype, melainotype

1854 J. A. Cutting, ambrotype

1855 J. C. Maxwell, isolation of primary colours

1855 Poitevin, carbon-potassium bichromate print process (later Pouncy, Swan, Du Hauron)

1858 H. Anthony, ammonia-fumed albumen paper

1860 Collodion dry plate

1862 L. Ducos du Hauron, beam splitter camera for colour images

1865 Woodburytype photomechanical printing process

1868 Photolithography/collotype

1868 L. Ducos du Hauron, *Les Couleurs en Photographie*

1871 Liverpool Dry Plate Co., gelatin coated silver bromide printing paper

1873 H. W. Vogel, dye-sensitized orthochromatic collodion plates

1873 W. Willis, platinotype

1878 Gelatin silver bromide glass dry plate

1879 Photogravure

1880 W. de W. Abney, hydroquinone developer

1880 J. Eder and Toth, pyrocatechin developer

1882 H. B. Berkeley, use of sodium sulphite as a preservative for organic developing agents

1881 Half-tone screen

1883 J. Eder, developing-out chlorobromide paper

1884 Eastman, roll film system and machine coated printing paper

1884 Vogel-Ohbernetter, orthochromatic dry plate

1886 W. de W. Abney and P. E. Liesegang, aristotype gelatin silver chloride paper

1887 H. Goodwin, patent application for celluloid roll film

1887 G. Pizzighelli, platinum printing-out process

1888 Emulsion stripping paper roll film

1888 J. Carbutt, emulsion coated on celluloid sheets

1888 Developing-out paper, gelatin silver bromide

1888 Kodak camera, "You press the button—We do the rest."

1888 F. Hurter and V C. Driffield, actinograph

1888 M. Andresen, *p*-phenylenediamine developer

1889 H. Shawcross, Vandyke brown print process

1889 Eastman nitrocellulose roll film base

1890 Printing-out paper, gelatin silver chloride

1890 F. Hurter and V. C. Driffield, *Photographic Researches*

1890 Gelatin silver chloride gas light paper

1890 Platinum chloride paper

1891 L. Ducos du Hauron, Anaglyphs, 3-D photographs using red-green discrimination for separation

1891 M. Andresen, use of para-aminophenol, Rodinal, as developer

1891 A. Bogisch, metol developer

1891 F. Ives, Kromskop "one-shot" three-colour separation camera

1891 S. N. Turner, Kodak daylight loading film rolls

1891 G. Lippmann, wavelength interference colour system

1893 Baekeland, Velox silver chloride ammonia gaslight paper

1894 J. Joly, line screen additive colour images

1895 R. E. J. Liesegang, silver bleached away, dye image remains

1895 W. C. Roentgen, discovery of x-rays and radiography

1896 R. E. J. Liesegang, lenticular screen colour process

1899 T. Manly, ozotype carbon

1901 A. Eichengrun, cellulose acetate film base

1902 H. Luppo-Cramer, metal-hydroquinone developer

1902 Kodak gelatin anti-curl backing for film

1903 Agfa, panchromatic film

1905 K. Schinzel, dye destruction

1906 Finlaycolor additive screen plate

1906 F. C. L. Wratten and Wainwright, commercial panchromatic plates

1907 Lumière Brothers, Autochrome plate (1904 patents)

1907 B. Homolka, leuco dye colour development

1907 C. W. Piper and E. J. Wall, bromoil process
1908 Dufay, poured colour
1912 R. Fischer and H. Siegrist, colour couplers for dye formation
1914 A. Keller-Dorian, lenticular cinematographic system
1915 Technicolor dye imbibition motion picture film
1915 Kodachrome, subtractive 2-colour process, black-and white separation negatives.
1916 Agfacolor dyed varnish screen plate film
1919 Autotype Co., carbro print process
1920 H. Luppo-Cramer, desensitization
1921 Pako automated processing machine
1921 A. Bocage, x-ray tomographs of living subjects
1923 J. G. Capstaff Cine-Kodak reversal process motion picture film
1925 Dye imbibition
1928 Kodacolor lenticular colour motion picture film
1929 K. Jacobsohn, hypersensitization with ammonia and ammoniacal silver chloride
1930 Three-colour carbro print process
1932 Agfa lenticulated film
1932 B. Gaspar, Gasparcolor dye bleach motion picture film
1935 L. Mannes and L. Godowsky, Kodachrome 16-mm movie film, three-colour subtractive reversal film, colour couplers added to developers (1936—35 mm, 1938—sheets)
1935 Gasparcolor opaque dye-bleach printing material
1936 Agfacolor Neu, tripack coupler incorporated
1938 N. F Mott and R. W. Gurney, theory of the latent image
1938 C. Carlson and O. Kornei, dry powder pigment image-transfer copy system
1939 A. Rott and E. Weyde, diffusion-transfer copying systems
1939 Agfacolor negative-positive colour printing process
1940 Ilford multigrade variable contrast paper
1941 Kodacolor dispersed-coupler colour negative film
1942 Ilford, phenidone developing agent
1943 Kodacolor Aero dispersed-coupler colour reversal film
1946 Ektachrome reversal sheet film, user processed
1946 Kodak Dye Transfer print process
1947 D. Gabor, theory of holography
1948 E. H. Land, Polaroid black-and-white peel-apart diffusion-transfer material
1948 Kodak cellulose triacetate safety film, nonnitrate base
1948 W. T. Hanson, Kodak integral mask colour negative film
1950 Eastman colour negative and print motion picture films
1950 DuPont polyethylene terephthalate (PET) film support
1955 Kodak Type C Ektacolor paper
1955 Kodak Type R Ektachrome paper
1963 Polacolor peel-apart colour diffusion transfer
1972 Polaroid SX-70 integral diffusion transfer colour material
1976 Kodak Instant Print film
1978 Polavision Self-Processing diffusion-transfer 8-mm additive (screen) movie film
1979 Ilford Galerie paper

1979 Cibachrome "A" Pearl surface resin coated paper
1979 Olympus OM-2 Camera, which reads subject illumination on the film and controls exposure at the time it is made
1981 Ilford XP-400 black-and-white film makes use of colour technology and can be processed in proprietary XP1 chemistry or C-41
1981 Kodak Ektachrome 160 movie film introduced in 8mm and 16-mm formats, requires new EM-26 process
1981 3M high-speed artificial-light tungsten colour film having an ASA rating of 640
1981 Kodak Ektaflex PCT one-solution colour print making system for both colour negatives and transparencies
1981 Improved Cibachrome A-II material utilizing a P-30 chemistry makes home processing easier
1982 Kodak Disc-Film camera, film, and processing system
1982 Sony Mavigraphy, a new electronic photographic system
1983 A revolutionary T-grain emulsion system makes it possible to introduce a new Kodak 1000-speed colour film
1983 Polaroid Autoprocess 35-mm Transparency system consisting of one colour and two black-and-white films, along with a compact low-contrast manual processor, slide mounter, and mounts
1983 Polaroid Polaprinter capable of making instant full colour prints in about one minute
1982 Technidol developer for use with Kodak Technical Pan 2415 film
1984 Kodak Camcorder (camera-recorder) 8-mm cassette video system
1984 Vivitar Autofocus 200 AF lens, which works by comparing the images formed by light passing through the lens, measuring displacement of different clusters of light
1984 Kodak Elite Fine-Art Paper, a premium black-and white enlarging paper
1986 Video cameras (camcorders) by RCA, GE, Chinon, and others
1987 Kodak T-Max developer for use with T-Max (T-grain) and other black-and-white films
1989 Kodak Ektapress 1600 colour negative film capable of exposure indexes up to 3200 with normal processing, and 6400 with modified processing
1991 Kodak Photo CD

2.2 ADVANCES IN PHOTOGRAPHIC TECHNOLOGY

1200s Simple glass lenses were introduced.
1472 Leonardo da Vinci: discovered the multicoloured nature of white light.
1676 Sturm, J.C.: Portable camera obscura with reflex mirror and focusing lens.
1704 Newton, Sir Isaac: Published *Opticks* in which he presented his discoveries in optics and elaborated on his corpuscular theory of light.

1725 Schulze, J.H.: Experiments on light sensitivity of silver salts: contact images (from stencils) on liquid mixtures of chalk and silver nitrate in a bottle; no fixing.

1758 Dolland, John: Invented the achromatic lens.

1777 Lichtenberg, G.C.: Developed electrostatic discharge patterns with dry powder.

1777 Scheele, C.W.: Blackening of silver chloride in the violet and the blue of the spectrum quicker than by other colours.

1800 Herschel, Sir William: Discovered infrared radiation.

1800 Wedgwood, T.: Contact copying of silhouettes, leaves, etc., on leather sensitized with silver nitrate; no fixing.

1801 Ritter, J.W.: Blackening of silver chloride by ultraviolet radiation.

1815-1820 Brewster, Sir David: Invented the optical system of the future parlor stereoscope.

1816 Niépce, J. Nicéphore: Camera photographs on paper sensitized with silver chloride; partially fixed.

1819 Herschel, Sir John F. W.: Discovery of thiosulphates and of the solution of silver halides by "hypo."

1822-1825 Niépce, J. Nicéphore: Copying of engravings on glass, zinc, and pewter sensitized with bitumen. Further attempts at direct photography.

1826 Niépce, J. Nicéphore: First photograph from nature on pewter sensitized with bitumen (exposure 8 hours). Bellows for photographic camera; iris diaphragm.

1827 Niépce, J. Nicéphore: First prints from etched heliographic plates.

1833 Florence, Hercules: Worked with paper sensitized with silver salts and coined the word *photography* in Brazil, but his achievements were not widely recognized until 1973.

1835 Talbot, W.H. Fox: "Photogenic drawings," copied on paper sensitized with silver chloride; fixed with potassium iodide or by prolonged washing in salt water. Also tiny camera photographs.

1835-1837 Daguerre, L.J.M.: Daguerreotype (direct photography on silvered copper plates with a silver iodide surface); development of the latent image by mercury vapour, 1837, fixing with salt solution.

1838 Morse, S.F.B.: Demonstrated his telegraph system.

1839 Bayard, H.: Direct positive photographs on paper (silver chloride paper blackened by light, then impregnated with potassium iodide and exposed in the camera).

1839 Daguerre, L.J.M.: Publication of working instructions for the daguerreotype by the French Government.

1839 Experimental photographic portraits in France and U.S.A.

1839 Herschel, Sir John F.W.: Generally credited with the first use of the word "photography." (See 1833.) Independent invention of a photographic process in glass.

1839 Ponton, Mungo: Light sensitivity of a paper impregnated with potassium bichromate—the basis of many printing processes.

1839 Reade, J.B.: Photomicrographs in the solar microscope

on paper sensitized with silver nitrate and gallic acid (by printing out or by development with gallic acid); fixing with thiosulphate.

1839-1841 Donné, A.; Berres, Joseph; Grove, W. R.; Fizeau, H.L.: Transformation of daguerreotypes into etched printing plates.

1840 Draper, J.W.: First successful daguerreotype portrait.

1840 Fizeau, H.L.: Gold toning of daguerreotypes.

1840 Goddard, J.F: Use of bromide for the acceleration of daguerreotype plates.

1840 Petzval, J.: Portrait lens (first application of calculation for the investigation of a lens type).

1840 Soleil, J.B.F.: Actinometer for exposure time determination.

1840 Wolcott, A.: Patents for mirror camera in U.S.A.

1840 Wolcott, A.: Opened world's first photographic portrait studio in New York.

1841 Beard, R.: Opened first photographic portrait studio in Europe.

1841 Claudet, A.: Red light for dark room.

1841 Talbot, W.H. Fox: Calotype process (negatives on silver iodide paper impregnated with silver nitrate and gallic acid; development of the latent image by gallic acid, positive prints from these paper negatives).

1842 Herschel, Sir John F.W.: Ferro-prussiate paper and other processes using iron salts.

1843 Claudet, A.F.J.: Use of painted backgrounds for portraiture.

1844 Fizeau, H.L., and Foucault, L.: Discovery of reciprocity failure on daguerreotypes; photographic photometry.

1844 Hunt, R.: Ferrous oxalate process, ferrous sulphate development.

1844 Talbot, W.H. Fox: Published part I of the *Pencil of Nature*, the first photographically illustrated book.

1845 Martens, F. von: Panoramic camera for daguerreotypes

1847 Blanquart-Evrard, L.D.: Modification of Calotype process.

1847 Mathieu, P.E.: Gold toning of positive prints on paper.

1847 Niépce de St. Victor, C.F.A.: Negatives on glass by the albumen process.

1848 Becquerel, Edmond: Attempts at colour photography (heliochrouy) on silver plates that were incompletely chlorinated.

1848 Niépce, A.: Albumen process.

1849 Brewster, Sir David: Lenticular stereoscope prototype. Introduced 1851. Suggests binocular camera, prototype 1853.

1850 Blanquart-Evrard, L.D.: Albumen paper for positive prints.

1850 Humphrey, S.D.: Publication of the first photographic journal: *The Daguerreian Journal*, New York.

1850 Le Gray, G.: Waxed paper process.

1851 Archer, F.S., and Fry, P.W.: Ambrotypes (negative collodion-on-glass photos with black background giving positive effect).

1851 Archer, F.S.: Wet-collodion process.

1851 Blanquart-Evrard, L.D.: Prints by development.

1851 Claudet, A.: Duboscq, J.: Animated photographs (in Zoetrope and Phenakistoscope) suggested.

1851 Dodero: Portraits on visiting cards, popularized by Disdéri.

1851 Regnault, V: Use of pyrogallol as developer (physical development).

1851 Talbot, W.H. Fox: Photograph of an object in rapid movement by using an electric spark.

1852 Laussedat, A.: Photography applied to surveying.

1852 Lemercier, Lerebours, Barreswil, and Davanne: Photolithography with halftones on grained stone sensitized with bitumen.

1852 Martin, A.A.: Positive-looking images by the wet-collodion process on a blackened metal support (ferrotypes).

1852 Talbot, W.H. Fox: Insolubilization of bichromated gelatin by light; first experiments with halftone heliogravure.

1852-1853 Delves, J.; Highley, S.; Shadbolt, G.: Photomicrographs by the wet-collodion process.

1853 Dancer, J.B.: Prototype of stereo-camera with two lenses.

1853 Dancer, J.B.: Microphotographs by the wet-collodion process .

1853 Gaudin, M.A.A.: Use of potassium cyanide as fixing agent for silver images; experiments with gelatin as carrier for silver images.

1853 Martin, A.A.: Tintype process (wet collodion).

1854 Brébisson, A. de: Salted paper with starch, for positive prints .

1854 Cutting, J. Ambrose: Patented ambrotype process.

1854 Melhuish, A.J. and Spencer, J.B.: Roll-holders for sensitive paper negatives.

1854 Nègre, C.: Photo engravings giving halftone with bitumen-coated steel plate.

1855 Lafon de Camarsac, P.M.: Photographs on enamel and porcelain (burnt-in).

1855 Niépce de St. Victor, C.FA.: Heliogravure with bitumen on steel.

1855 Poitevin, A.L.: Photolithography on stone sensitized with bichromated gelatin, glue, albumen or gum—principle of collotype; first attempts to obtain *carbon* prints.

1855 Relandin: Roller-blind shutter mounted on the lens.

1855 Taupenot, J.M.: Negatives on collodio-albumen dry plates prepared in advance and requiring only a complementary sensitization .

1856 Martin, A.A.: Dry tintype process.

1856 Norris, R. Hill: Collodion dry plates preserved with gum arabic or gelatin put on the market.

1856 Pretsch, P: Photogalvanography (halftone intaglio copper printing plates by galvanoplastic moulding from bichromated gelatin reliefs).

1857 Grubb, Thomas: Aplanat lens.

1857 Woodward, J.J.: Solar enlarger.
1858 Tournachon, G.F. ("Nadar"): Photography from the air in a free-floating balloon.
1859 Asser, E.J. and James, Sir H.: Photozincography.
1859 Bunsen, R., and Roscoe, H.E.: Use of magnesium to provide artificial light.
1860 Joubert, F.: "Phototype" (eollotype).
1860 Willéme, F.: Photosculpture.
1861 England, W.: Focal plane shutter.
1861 Fargier, A.: Halftone pigment images on bichromated gelatin with transparent support, exposed from the back.
1861 Maxwell, J. Clerk: Three-colour separation, and colour synthesis by multiple projection.
1861 Russell, C.: Dry-collodion plates preserved with tannin.
1862 Leahy, Thomas, and Russell, C.: Alkaline developer (pyrogallol-ammonia) for chemical development; reversal by dissolving the first negative and development of the remaining silver salt.
1864 Bolton, W.B., and Sayce, B.J.: First workable collodion emulsion.
1864 Ducos du Hauron, L.: Patent for an apparatus for animated photography (camera and projector) made by J. Duboscq.
1864 Swan, Sir Joseph W.: First successful carbon process (with double transfer).
1864 Woodbury, W.B.: Multiplication of carbon prints by moulding (Woodbury-type).
1865 Simpson, G. Wharton: Positive collodio-chloride emulsion for printing-out papers, made by J.B. Obernetter (1868).
1865 White, W.: Magnesium flash powder.
1866 Sanchez, M., and Laurent, J.: Baryta coating of photographic papers.
1866 Steinheil, A.: Aplanat lens (rectilinear).
1867 Cook, H.: Opera-glass camera and plate change-box for dry collodion plates.
1868 Albert, J.: Perfected collotype (use of glass plates as supports).
1868 Cros, C.: Principle of three-colour separation and synthesis.
1868 Ducos du Hauron, L.: Three-colour photography and the various methods of achieving it; subtractive colour synthesis.
1868 Harrison, W.H.: Experiments with positive silver bromide gelatin emulsion for chemical development.
1869 Ost, A.: Citric acid stabilization of printing-out papers.
1870 Dagron, P.R.P.: Use of miniature photographs for the pigeon post during the Siege of Paris.
1871 Maddox, R.L.: First gelatin dry plates. Extremely slow. Improved by J. Burgess (1873), R. Kennett (1874) and C. Bennett (1878).
1872 Gillot, C.: Line blocks on zinc, using the etching technique of F. Gillot (1850).
1873 Mawdsley, P.: Gelatin bromide paper for negatives and

positives.

1873 Vogel, H.: Dye sensitization for the green (basis of orthochromatic plates).

1873 Willis, W: Platinum paper for development (sold commercially in 1878 after various improvements).

1873-1874 Johnston, J.; King, J.: Silver bromide gelatin emulsion (negative) prepared with excess bromide and washed before coating.

1874 Janssen, P.J.: Photographic revolver for the chronophotographic study of the Venus transit.

1875 Warnerke, L.: Stripping-film paper on reels in a rollholder for 100 exposures.

1876 The Liverpool Dry Plate Co. began manufacture of R. Kennett's gelatin dry plates.

1877 Carey-Lea, M.: Ferrous oxalate developer.

1877-1885 Muybridge, E.: Study of the movement of animals by instantaneous photography and chronophotography.

1878 Monckhoven, D.C.E. van: Preparation of silver bromide gelatin emulsions in the presence of ammonia.

1878 Swan, J.W., and Bennett, C.: Increase in the speed of silver bromide gelatin emulsions by ripening in a neutral medium.

I878 Wratten, F.C.L.: "Noodling" of silver bromide gelatin emulsions before washing.

1879 Kliç, K.: Photogravure on copper by transfer of a carbon print after graining with resin.

1879 Swan, J.W., also Eastman, G.: Machine for coating plates.

1880 Abney, Sir W. de W.: Use of hydroquinone as developer.

1881 Cros, C.: Dyeing of gelatin by imbibition ("hydrotypy").

1881 Eder, J.M., and Pizzighelli, G.: Silver chloride gelatin emulsion (positive) for chemical development.

1881 Horgan, S.: Halftone photomechanical reproduction process.

1881 Pumphrey, A.: Magazine camera (for gelatin sheet film).

1882 Attout, P.A. and Clayton, J.: Commercial manufacture of orthochromatic silver bromide gelatin plates.

1882 Abney, Sir W. de W.: Silver chloride gelatin emulsion for printing-out papers manufactured commercially in 1886 by Liesegang.

1882 Berkeley, H.B.: Use of sodium sulphite in developers.

1882 Meisenbach, G.: Commercial production of halftone blocks (line screen turned at 90° in the middle of the exposure).

1882-1896 Marey, E.J.: Chronophotography on fixed plates and on movable films (photographs in rapid succession at equal time intervals).

1883 Farmer, E.H.: Single-bath reducer (with ferricyanide and thiosulphate).

1884 Kayser, H.: Plate changing magazine.

1884 Nipkow, P.: First described the essential elements of a viable TV system.

1885 Urie, John, sen. and jun.: Patent for automatic positive printing machine.

1886 Ives, F.E.: Halftone blocks with crossed screen and square diaphragm.

1886 Urie, John, sen. and jun.: Patent for continuous positive print processing machine.

1887 Bausch, E.: Central shutter with blades forming, also an iris diaphragm.

1887 Goodwin, H.: Patent (granted only in 1898) for the manufacture of celluloid rollfilm coated with silver bromide gelatin emulsion.

1887 Hertz, Heinrich: The father of wireless communication; demonstrated the radiation of electromagnetic waves.

1887 Pizzighelli, G.: Platinum paper for printing-out.

1888 Anschutz, O.: Patented focal plane shutter with 1/1000 second exposure time.

1888 Carbutt, J.: Silver bromide gelatin coated celluloid sheet film.

1888 Eastman Kodak Co.: Introduction of the first "Kodak" roll film camera.

1888 Hurter, F. and Driffield, V.: Patented actinograph, a slide-rule type exposure calculator.

1888-1889 Andresen, M.: Use of para-phenylenediamine and Eikonogen as developers.

1889 Edison, T.A.: Use of flexible Eastman film for Kinetoscope pictures.

1889 Enjalbert, T.E.: Portrait automaton for ferrotypes.

1889 Lainer, A.: Stabilization of fixers with bisulphites.

1889 Namias, R.: Acid permanganate reducer.

1889 Rudoloph, P.: First anastigmat lens (Protar) introduced by Zeiss.

1890 Bonnet, G.: Bichromated glue process for block-making (so-called "enamel" process).

1890 Hurter, F., and Driffield, V.C.: Scientific investigation of emulsion characteristics; creation of photographic photometry and sensitometry.

1891 Andresen, M.: Use of para-aminophenol as developer.

1891 Bogisch, A.: Use of metal, glycin and diaminophenol as developers.

1891 Edison, T.A.: Kinetoscope giving the illusion of movement by viewing images representing phases of a short scene.

1891 Lippmann, G.: Colour photography by the interference method .

1891 Turner, S.N.: Daylight-loading film rolls (Kodak).

1892 Ives, F.E.: One-shot colour camera.

1893 von Hoegh, E.: First double anastigmat lens (Dagor) introduced by Goerz.

1893 Schumann, V.: Emulsions with negligible gelatin content, sensitive for the extreme ultraviolet.

1893 Taylor, H.D.: Anastigmatic objectives with three uncemented lenses (Cooke lens).

1894 Ives, F.E.: Patents photochromoscope, later called "Kromskop," viewer for seeing single or stereoscopic photographs in colour (invented 1892).

1894 Rouillé-Ladevéze, A.: Gum-bichromate prints for picto-

rial photography.
1895 Kliç, K.: Intaglio screen photogravure and rotogravure introduced. (Invented 1890.)
1895 Lumière, A. and L.: Cinematograph.
1895 Roentgen, W.C.: Discovery of x-rays and of radiography.
1896 Méliès, G.: Directing of films; cinematographic effects and illusions.
1897 Braun, K.F.: Invented the cathode ray tube (CRT).
1898 Acres, Birt: First narrow-gauge cine film (17.5 mm., Birtac camera).
1900 Lumière, A. and L.: "Photorama" for the taking and the projection of panoramic pictures of 360°.
1900-1905 Von Bronk, O.: Described electrolytic electrophotography with a photoconductor.
1901 Eichengrün, A.: Safety films from cellulose acetate.
1901 Gaumont, L.: Synchronization of a cinematograph with a phonograph.
1901 Marconi, M.G.: Made the first transatlantic wireless transmission .
1901 Pulfrich, C.: Stereocomparator for the accurate exploitation of stereo pairs in terrestrial photogrammetry.
1902 Deckel, Fr.: Compound shutter.
1902 Deville, E.: Principles of an apparatus for stereophotogrammetric restitution.
1902 Eastman Kodak Company: Gelatin backing on films to prevent curl (commercially introduced); daylight development tank.
1902 Lüppo-Cramer, H.: Metol-hydroquinone developer.
1902 Rudolph, P.: Tessar anastigmat lens introduced by Zeiss.
1902 Traube, A.: Ethyl Red used as colour sensitizer; this was the first sensitizer of the isocyanine series.
1904 Fleming, J.A.: Invented the diode vacuum tube rectifier and detector.
1904 Goerz, C.: Pneumatic lens shutter using one set of overlapping blades for the shutter and the iris diaphragm.
1904 Johnston, W.: Patented panoramic camera design that was later labelled *circuit* camera.
1904 König, E., and Homolka, B.: Ortho and panchromatic sensitizers (Orthochrome, Pinachrome, Pinacyanol).
1904 Korn and Glatzel: Phototelegraphy.
1904 Rawlins, G.E.: Fatty ink processes (*oil prints*) applied to artistic photography.
1905 Brehm, F.: Patented first cirkut camera to be commercially manufactured.
1906 Courtet, E. (pseudonym Cohl): Animated films.
1906 DeForest, Lee: Invented the triode vacuum tube amplifier.
1906 Wratten and Wainwright Ltd.: First commercial panchromatic plates.
1907 Goldschmidt, R.B.: Photographic reduction of documents for library use.
1907 Homolka, B.: Colour development with leuco dyes.
1907 Lumière, A. and L.: Autochrome plate for colour pho-

tography introduced.
1907 Smith, C.A., and Urban, C.: Kinemacolor, first commercial additive two-colour cine process.
1907 Welbourne Piper, C., and Wall, E.J.: Bromoil process.
1908 Belin, E.: Phototelegraphy on telephone lines.
1908 Clerc, L.P: Theory of the photogravure screen.
1910 Keller-Dorian, A.: Patent for lenticular colour process for cinematography.
1910 Dufay, L.: Regular screen process of additive colour photography.
1910 Goldberg, E.: Moulded neutral grey wedges for sensitometry
1911 Lauste, E.A.: First experiments in talking films.
1912 Armstrong, E.H.: Developed the electronic oscillator.
1912 Deckel, Fr.: Compur shutter introduced.
1912 Fischer, R.: Multi-contrast paper.
1912 Fischer, R., and Siegrist,H.: Colour development based on formation of indamine and indophenol dyes (later employed in three-colour photography).
1912 Gaumont, L.: Three-colour cinematography by simultaneous additive synthesis.
1914 Eastman Kodak Co.: First Kodachrome process (two colour subtractive).
1919 Adams, E.Q., and Haller, H.L.: Discovery of cryptocyanine, the first practical sensitizer for infra-red.
1920 Lüppo-Cramer, H.: Desensitization.
1920 Pope, Sir William J., Mills, W.H., and Hamer, Miss F.M.: Constitution of the colour sensitizers of the cyanine group.
1921 Belin, E.: Transmission of pictures by wireless.
1921 Bocage, A.: Radiographic tomography of living objects.
1921 Duclaux, J., and Jeantet, P.: Sensitization for the far ultraviolet by putting a fluorescent layer on the emulsion.
1923 Eastman Kodak Co.: Reversal processing of 16-mm film, leading to widespread amateur cinematography.
1923 Koegel, G.: Diazo prints developed with ammonia vapour.
1923 König, W.: Preparation of di- and tri-carbocyanines, sensitizers for the extreme red and the near infrared.
1924 Barnack, O.: Leica camera using 35-mm film, manufactured by Leitz.
1924 Sheppard, S.E., and Punnelt, R.F.: Discovery and identification of active impurities in gelatin, which led to the preparation of very rapid emulsions.
1924 Zworykin, V.R.: Invented the Iconoscope TV camera tube.
1925 Séguin, A., and L.: Practical use of a condenser discharge in a rare gas for the photography of very rapid movements.
1927 Beginning of universal use of sound films.
1928 Arens, H., and Eggert, J.: Density surfaces for various types of emulsion.
1928 Commercial microfilming on 16-mm film in rotary camera.
1928 Eastman Kodak Co.: Lenticular additive colour amateur motion picture film. First Kodacolor film.
1928 Franke & Heidecke: Rolleiflex twin-lens reflex camera

introduced.

1928 Hamer, Miss F.M.: Polymethine sensitizers derived from benzothiazoles with alkyl substitution on the middle carbon.

1929 Ostermeir, J.: Flashbulb: Combustion of aluminum wire or foil in oxygen in a sealed bulb.

1931 Schmidt, B.: Catadioptric lens with large aperture.

1932 Technicolor Corp.: First full-length colour motion picture films produced using the imbibition colour transfer process.

1932 Western Electric Instrument Corp.: Weston Universal 617 photoelectric exposure meter.

1935 Birr, E.J. (Agfa): Triazaindolizines (azaindene) emulsion stabilizers .

1935 Brooker, L.G.S., and Keyes, G.H.: Preparation of tetra- and penta-carbocyanines.

1935 Heisenberg, E.: Emulsion for direct positives and prints, without inversion of a provisional negative.

1935 Laporte, M.: Electronic flash with white light.

1935 Mannes, L.D., and Godowsky, L. (Kodak): Subtractive three-colour separation with superimposed emulsion layers, the colour couplers added to the developers, and colour separation obtained by controlled differential dye bleaching. (Early Kodachrome process).

1935 Merocyanine spectral sensitizers discovered independently by J.D. Kendall (llford) and L.G.S. Brooker (Kodak).

1935 Selenyi, P.: Described dry powder development of charge patterns formed on an insulating layer.

1936 Kine: Exakta 35-mm single-lens reflex camera

1936 Koslowski, R.: Discovers gold sensitization of silver halide emulsions, but discovery is kept a trade secret by Agfa until 1945.

1936 Land, E.H.: Stereoscopic projection with two projectors equipped with polarizing filters; viewers used polarizing spectacles.

1936 Strong, J.: Reflection-diminishing coatings with insoluble fluorides on lens surfaces.

1936 Wilmanns, G., Kumetat, K., Frohlich, A., and Schneider, W. (Agfa): Fat-tail couplers incorporated in the emulsion layers of colour films. Used in Agfacolor films.

1937 Mees, C.E.K. (Kodak): Supersensitization using the combination of two sensitizing dyes giving higher sensitivity than the sum of their individual effects.

1938 Carlson, Chester F.: Invented electrostatic electrophotography, later called xerography.

1938 Kodak: Super 620 camera with automatic photocell exposure control.

1938 Mannes, L.D., Godowsky, L., and Wilder, L. (Kodak): Improved Kodachrome process based on selective reexposure.

1938 Mott, N.F., and Gurney, R.W.: Theory of latent image formation .

1938 Trivelli, A.P.H., and Smith, W.F (Kodak): Independently

discover gold sensitization of silver halide emulsions.
1938-1939 Staehle, H.C. (Kodak): Cardboard mount for 35mm colour slides.
1939 Agfacolor negative-positive colour printing process.
1939 Dumont: first commercial TV sets.
1939 Edgerton, H.E.: Improvement in electronic flash lamps.
1939 James, T.H.: Investigations of the kinetics of development.
1939 Jones, L.A.: Experimental basis of the standardization of the sensitometry of negative emulsions.
1939 Leermakers, J.A., Yackel, E.C., and Hewitson, E.H. (Kodak): Improved gold sensitization using silver halide emulsions made with inert gelatin and sensitized with thiosulphate, thiocyanate, and a water-soluble gold salt.
1940 Ardenne, M. von: Investigation of the structure of developed images with an electron microscope.
1940 Weisberger, A. (Kodak): Low allergenic alkysulphonamidoalkyl substituted phenylenediamine colour developers.
1941 High-resolution plates permitting 750-times enlargement.
1941 Niet, A., and Russell, F (Kodak): Thiocyanate ripened silver halide emulsions.
1942 Atanasoff, J.V., and Berry, C.: Built the first electronic digital computer.
1942 Carroll, B.H., and Allen, C.F.H. (Kodak): Quaternary ammonium salt development accelerators used to increase sensitivity.
1942 Gaspar, B.: Oxonol filter and backing dyes.
1942 Kendall, J.D.: Patent on Phenidone, a new developing agent (1-phenyl-3-pyrazolidone).
1942 Rott, A. (Gevaert): Reversal images produced by the silver salt diffusion image transfer process. Also discovered independently by E. Weyde at Agfa. Evolved into document copying and instant photography.
1942 Silver halide-sensitized zinc plates for rapid photolithography.
1943 Jelley, E.E., and Vittum, P.W (Kodak): Oil-in-water dispersions of nondiffusing couplers. Process currently used in most incorporated-coupler colour materials.
1944 Gaspar, B.: Colour separation by sensitivity differential. System used in most colour print materials.
1944 Stauffer, R.E., Smith, W.F, and Trivelli, A.P.H. (Kodak): High contrast images produced by the hydrazine effect.
1945 Multicontrast papers with the contrast depending on the colour of the exposing light.
1946 Back, F (Zoomar Corp.): Designed zoom lens or 16-mm motion-picture cameras.
1946 Blackner, L.L., Brown, FM., and Kunz, C.J.: Rapid processing and projection of images 15 seconds after taking.
1946 Evans, R.M.: Introduced the photofinishing concept that the total light reflected from each print should integrate approximately to a neutral hue.
1946 Ilford, Kodak: Improved nuclear track materials for

recording nuclear particles.
1946-1950 Kodak/Time-Life scanner for halftone separation negatives.
1947 Blake, R.K., Stanton, W.A., and Schulze, F (DuPont): Polyethylene glycols used as development modifiers to increase sensitivity and contrast.
1947 Gabor, D: The theory of holography which became feasible after the introduction of lasers in 1960.
1947 Magnetic recording begins to replace photographic sound recording in motion picture films.
1948 Bardeen, J., Brattain, W., and Shockley, W.: Transistors, making miniature photocells and microelectronic circuits possible.
1948 Battelle Memorial Institute introduced the amorphous selenium photoconductor (Bixby, W.E.), corona charging (Walkup, L.E.), two-component dry xerographic development (Walkup, L.E. and Wise, E.N.) and electrostatic toner transfer to plain paper (Schaffert, R.M.).
1949 General introduction of safety cellulose ester film base for 35-mm motion picture films.
1949 Zeiss Contax S 35-mm single-lens reflex camera with pentaprism for eye-level viewing.
1950 Fallesen, G.E. (Kodak): Internal-image emulsion reversal process.
1950 Haloid-Xerox flat plate xerographic camera for plain paper copies and lithographic printing plates.
1950 Hanson, W.T. (Kodak): Coloured couplers used for integral masking .
1950 Kendall, W.B., and Hill, G. (Kodak): Autopositive materials, based on Herschel reversal, comprising fogged silver chloride emulsions containing a desensitizer.
1950 Norwood, D.: Incident-light exposure meter with a hemispherical light diffuser.
1950 RCA (Forgue, S.V., Goodrich, R.R., and Weimer, P.K.): Introduced the Vidicon TV camera tube.
1950 Russell, H.D., Yackel, E.C., and Bruce, J.S.: Principles of stabilization processing.
1950 Sprague, R.H. (Kodak): Sulphosubstituted cyanine dyes.
1951 Hanson, W.T., and Groet, N.H. (Kodak): Incorporated coupler colour negative film having an improved sensitivity graininess ratio, produced by double coated emulsion layers having the same spectral sensitivities but different overall sensitivities, with the more sensitive emulsion containing a low concentration of coupler. Used in Eastman Color Negative Motion-Picture Film.
1951 Ives, C.E. (Kodak): Improved internal-image reversal process using hydrazine fogging agents.
1951 Brooker, L.G.S., and Keyes, G.H. (Kodak): Solubilized merocyanine dyes.
1951 Davey, E.P., and Knott, E.B. (Kodak): Halide conversion internal-image emulsions.
1952 Lowe, W.G., Jones, J.E., and Roberts, H.E. (Kodak): Sulphur plus gold plus reduction sensitization.
1952 Yutzy, H.C., and Yackel, E.C.: Colloid image transfer

process used in the Kodak Verifax document copying process .

1953 Haloid-Xerox Copyflo xerographic microfilm enlarger.

1953 Miller, C.E., and Clark, B.L.: Thermal imaging system of the type used in the 3M Thermofax document copying process.

1953 NTSC standard for colour TV was announced.

1954 Minsk, L.M.: Photosensitive polyvinylcinnamate polymers used in photoengraving, lithography, and in the preparation of printed circuits. (Kodak Photo Resist).

1954 Univac: 1103 digital computer with magnetic-core memory.

1954 Young, C.J. and Grieg, H.G., (RCA): Demonstrated the Electrofax xerographic document copying process; expendable spectrally sensitized zinc oxide photoconductor and magnetic brush development.

1955 Carroll, B.H., and Spence, J. (Kodak): Use of acid substituted cyanine dyes to reduce unsensitizing of incorporated coupler emulsions.

1955 Haloid-Xerox: Xeroradiography with aerosol development.

1955 Poly (ethyleneterephthalate) film supports. (DuPont)

1955 Riester, O.H. (Agfa): Alkane sulphone synthesis of sulphoalkyl substituted cyanine dyes.

1955 Schouwenaars, M.A. (Gevaert): Reduction gold-fogged silver halide direct-positive emulsions.

1955 Yule, J.A.C., and Maurer, R.E. (Kodak Autoscreen Film): Prescreened *lith* films.

1955-1956 Logetronics enlarger/printer with optical feedback.

1956 Heseltine, D.W. (Kodak): Neopentylene infrared spectral sensitizers.

1956 Metcalfe, K.A., and Wright, R.D.: Described high-resolution xerographic development with toner particles dispersed in an insulating carrier liquid.

1956 Polyethylene resin coated paper supports. (RC papers)

1956 Russell, T.A. (Kodak): Simultaneous multilayer coating.

1957 Ginzberg, C.P. (Ampex): Developed the magnetic tape video recorder.

1958 Agfa: Planographic printing plates prepared using the silver salt diffusion transfer process.

1959 Kilby, J. (Texas Instruments) and Noyce, R.N.: Invented the integrated circuit chip.

1959 Russell, H.D., and Kun, C.J. (Kodak): Roller transport processing of radiographic films.

1959 3M:Filmac 100 Reader-Printer: zinc-oxide-photoconductor-coated foil and electrolytic development.

1959 Voigtlander: Optical compensation zoom lens for 35-mm single-lens-reflex camera.

1959 Xerox: 914 plain-paper xerographic document copier: radiant-heat toner fusing.

1959 Haloid, Xerox: Xerography – Introduction of the xerographic document copying system.

1960 Maiman, T.: Introduction of lasers, making holography possible.

1960-1965 Philips: Audio cassette magnetic tape recorder.
1961 Apeco: Document copier with zinc oxide paper and magnetic brush xerographic development.
1961 Hunt, H.D. (DuPont): Internal-image direct print emulsions containing a stannous salt halogen acceptor.
1961 Luckey, G.W., and Hoppe, J.C. (Kodak): Very high speed film using an image intensification system comprising a fogged internal-image silverchlorobromide emulsion blended with a surface-sensitized silver bromoiodide emulsion.
1961 Rogers, H.G. (Polaroid): Dye-developer colour image transfer process. Process used in Polacolor films.
1962 Dann, J.R., and Chechak, J.J. (Kodak): Thiopolymer sensitizers for silver-halide emulsions.
1962 IBM: Introduced magnetic disk computer program and data storage.
1962 SCM: Model 33 document copier with zinc oxide paper and liquid xerographic development.
1962 Williams, J., and Cossar, B.C. (Kodak): Thioether ripened silver-halide emulsions.
1962-1963 Bruning: Copytron 1000 microfilm enlarger with zinc oxide paper and magnetic brush xerographic development; precursor of the Model 2000 copier and the TCS lithographic plate maker.
1964 Sorensen, D., and Shepard, J. (3M Corp.): Photo thermographic system using silver halide, the silver salt of an organic acid, and a reducing agent.
1966 Barnes, J.C., and Rees, W.: 90-second processing of radiographic films using a hardening developer. Kodak XOMAT system.
1966 McBride, C.E. (Kodak): High-speed thioether ripened direct-print emulsions processed by photodevelopment.
1966 Weyerts, W.J., and Salminen, W.M. (Kodak): Improved dye-developer colour image transfer process using quaternary salts that form methylene bases. System used in Polacolor films.
1967 Dunn, J.S. (Kodak): Selenium plus gold sensitized silver halide emulsions.
1967 Gotze, A., and Riester, O. (Agfa): Fogged direct-positive emulsions containing phenylindole electron-accepting sensitizing dyes.
1967 Porter, H.D., James, T.H., and Lowe, W.G. (Kodak): Covered grain (core/shell) internal-image emulsions.
1967 Xerox: 2400 xerographic copier with hot-roller toner fusing.
1967 Xerox: 6500 xerographic colour document copier
1968 Bahnmuller, W.: Mechanism of iridium sensitization.
1968 Berriman, R.W (Kodak): Iridium doped reduction-gold fogged internal-image photobleach direct-positive silverhalide emulsions.
1968 Kitze, T.J. (Kodak): Incorporated developer papers containing a hardener precursor designed for rapid stabilization processing.
1968-1973 Phototypesetters for the graphic arts introduced by

Mergenthaler, Compugraphic, and others.

1968-1978 Scanners for graphic arts halftone separations introduced by Hell, Crossfield, and others.

1969 Barr, C.R., Thirtle, J.R., and Vittum, PW. (Kodak): Couplers that release developer inhibitors that improve graininess, DIR couplers. Used in Kodacolor II-type materials.

1969 Bell Labs (Boyle, W.S., and Smith, G.E.): Invented the charge-coupled device (CCD) photocell array.

1969 Brooker, L.G.S., and Van Lare, E. (Kodak): Imidazoquinoxaline electron-accepting spectral sensitizers.

1969 Morgan, D., and Shely, B. (3M Corp.): Improved photothermographic materials using silver halide, the silver salt of an organic acid, and a reducing agent in which the silver halide is formed *in situ* by reacting halide ions with the silver salt of the organic acid.

1970 IBM: xerographic copier with an organic photoconductor.

1970 Illingsworth, B.I. (Kodak): Reduction-gold fogged monodispersed photobleach direct-positive silver-halide emulsions.

1971 3M: xerographic copier using monocomponent developer

1972 James, T.H., Babcock, T.A., and Lewis, W.C. (Kodak): Hydrogen sensitization.

1972 Kodak: 110-film format and camera.

1972 Kodak: Three-solution rapid process for colour papers. System used for processing Ektacolor papers.

1972 Land, E.H. (Polaroid): SX-70 camera and integral colour image transfer system.

1972 Philips: videodisc with laser and photodiode readout; precursor of the compact disk (CD).

1972 Schwan, J.A., and Graham, J.L. (Kodak): Spectrally sensitized colour films designed to be exposed under several types of illumination. Universal sensitization.

1973 Evans, FJ. (Kodak): High speed internal-image core/shell silver-halide emulsions for use in the internal-image reversal process.

1975 Fleckenstein, L.J, and Figueras, J. (Kodak): Immobile sulphonamidophenol dye-release compounds of the type used in Kodak Instant Print Film.

1975 IBM: Model 3R00 xerographic computer; scanning HeNe laser exposure.

1975 Kodak: Ektaprint 100 xerographic document copier; belt-form aggregate-type organic photoconductor (Light, W.L., and Dulmage, W.J.), flash exposure, recirculating document feeder and conductive magnetic brush development.

1977 Kodak: Ektavolt organic photoconducting films.

1978 Polaroid: Sonar ultrasound rangefinding system.

1979 Canon: Sure Shot camera with infra-red rangefinding system .

1980 Nippon: Sheet Glass introduced with Selfoc gradient-index optics array.

1981 Sony: electronic still camera and thermal dye sublimation printing process.

1982 Kodak: Disk film format and camera.

1983 Canon: digital electronics copier with document scanner and xerographic printer.

1983 Canon: LBP-CX xerographic computer printer with semiconductor laser.

1983 Canon: personal xerographic copier with photoconductor, charged wires, and developer in a replaceable cartridge.

1983 Improved high-contrast emulsions containing arylacylhydrazide derivatives. Used in graphic arts films such as Kodak Ultratec Film.

1984 Abbott, T.I., and Jones, C.G.: Improved radiographic films containing high-aspect ratio spectrally sensitized silver-halide grains. Used in Kodak T-Mat Radiographic films.

1984 Bando, S., Shibahara, Y., and Ishimaru, S. (Fuji): Improved high-speed octahedral silver-bromoiodide double-structured grains having a silver-bromide core and a silver-bromoiodide shell.

1984 Epson and Casio: xerographic computer printers using liquid crystal (LCD) arrays with gradient-index optics.

1984 Kofron, J.T., Booms, R.E., Jones, C.G., Haefner, J.A., Wilgus, H.S., and Evans, F.J. (Kodak): Incorporated coupler colour-negative films with improved speed/graininess characteristics resulting from the use of high-aspect-ratio tabular grain spectrally sensitized silver-halide emulsions. Used in Kodacolor negative films such as Kodacolor VR 1U00 Film introduced in 1983.

1984 Solberg, J.C., Piggin, R.H., and Wilgus, H.S. (Kodak): Improved high-speed tabular grain silver-bromoiodide emulsions with the iodide concentrated in discrete areas.

1986 Kodak: 1.4-million pixel CCD array.

1986 Kodak: Ektaprint 1392 computer xerographic printer with light-emitting diodes (LED's) and gradient-index optics.

1986 Kodak: Signature colour-proofing system for the graphic arts; organic photoconducting film and liquid xerographic developers.

1988 Fuji: Heat-developable colour-image-transfer photographic materials containing heat-decomposable alkali precursors and sulphonamidophenol dye-release compounds.

1988 Konica: Colour photothermographic image-transfer process using a colour developer precursor and immobile couplers that form diffusible dyes.

1989 Canon: CLC 500 Colour Copier with digital electronics.

1989 Kodak: 4-million pixel CCD array.

1990 Kodak: Kodak Ektacolor RA-4 rapid-access process for processing colour papers.

1990 Kodak: 35-mm Rapid Film Scanner; CCD array.

1991 Kodak: Professional Digital Camera System (DCS); colour CCD; fits Nikon F3 camera body.

1991 Kodak; Photo CD (compact disc) System.

1991 Kodak: XL 7700 Digital Continuous Tone Printer; thermal dye-sublimation transfer process.

2.3 The Polaroid Corporation: an outline history

The Polaroid Corporation celebrated its 50th anniversary in 1987. The following chronological history constitutes a brief look at some of the significant events in Polaroid's history.

1926 Edwin H. Land leaves Harvard after his freshman year to pursue his own work on light polarization.

1928 Land creates the first synthetic sheet polarizer.

1929 Land files the patent for the first synthetic polarizer on April 26. He returns to Harvard to further his studies and continue polarizer research.

1932 Edwin Land leaves Harvard and with Harvard physics section leader George Wheelwright, II, establishes the Land-Wheelwright Laboratories to continue research and to manufacture polarizers.

1933 Land-Wheelwright Laboratories is incorporated to manufacture polarizers and to continue research into applications of polarizers in sunglasses, photographic and microscopic filers, and automobile headlights. Land is issued the patent covering synthetic sheet polarizers formed of parallel oriented submicroscopic crystals embedded in plastic film. The product is known as J-sheet.

1934 Eastman Kodak signs a contract with Sheet Polarizer Co., Inc., to purchase light polarizers for the manufacture of photographic filters.

1935 Land displays his invention to a representative of the American Optical Company. The American Optical Company signs a license agreement to use the polarizers for the manufacture of sunglasses. At the end of 1935, the first polarizer advertisement appears in a scientific journal, and Land receives the Hood Medal from the Royal Photographic Society. Land and Wheelwright develop the Polariscope, which is used to detect strains in transparent materials like glass and certain plastics.

1937 The Polaroid Corporation is organized under the laws of Delaware on September 13,1937. Land and Wheelwright receive the entire issue of 2,500 shares of Class B stock and approximately 60% of the common stock.

1938 Polaroid produces drafting table lamps, desk lamps, dermatology lamps, and polariscopes. Utilizing polarizing sheets, the company introduces variable density windows. The first installation is made on the club car of a Union Pacific streamliner.

1939 Curved lenses for prescription polarized sunglasses are developed using the glass/polarizer/glass laminates, making it possible to manufacture ground-and-polished prescription spectacles. Polaroid's stereoscopic motion picture, *In Tune with Tomorrow*, is shown at the New York World's Fair as part of the Chrysler exhibit. The first year's film is in black and white; the second year's is in colour.

1940 Polaroid announces Vectograph 3-D pictures. The Vectograph represents the fusion of the company's original technology, the polarizer, with photography. Among other applications, Vectographs will be used for aerial reconnaissance surveys during the Second World War. Other products include optical goods, lighting equipment, 3-D picture viewer, polarized sheeting, variable density day glasses, study lamp, 3-D motion pictures and polarizers.

1941 The ability to produce stereoscopic motion pictures is adapted for the three-dimensional sound movies and optical bullets.

1942 Most of Polaroid's products are for the war effort. With the invasion of Guadacanal, aerial vectographs are used extensively for military reconnaissance.

1943 Polaroid produces variable-density goggles, dark-adaptor goggles, aviation goggles for Army and Navy flying personnel, and fog-free goggles, polarizing filters and nonpolarizing colored filters for use in gunsights, rangefinders, periscopes, binoculars, and other military instruments.

1944 Land conceives of the one-step photographic system. Only after three years of intensive work will Land and a group of Polaroid scientists and engineers produce the complete photographic system.

1945 A polarized, daylight driving visor is developed as a result of research into a polarizing system to eliminate glare from oncoming headlights.

1946 Research continues on one-step photography: a new method of colour motion picture processing (called Polacolor), and Vectography.

1947 Land announces the one-step process for producing finished photographs within one minute.

1948 The first Land camera, the Model 95, is sold in Boston at Jordan Marsh department store on November 26 for $89.50.

1949 Photographic sales of the Polaroid Land camera Model 95 for the first year exceed $5 million. Land hires Ansel Adams as a consultant.

1950 By 1950 more than 4,000 dealers throughout the United States sell Polaroid cameras, film, and accessories. A contract from the Signal Corps results in the Tell-tale, a film badge that records radiation over a period of time. The resulting radiation record is developed in 60 seconds.

1951 A print coater is added to black-and-white film. The print coater is a simple treatment for long-term image stability. The chemical components of the coater liquid neutralize any alkalinity and remove any residual processing reagent left on the sheet. The coater solution then dries to a hard coating that protects the print from atmospheric contaminants. Type 1001 Land film for radiography is introduced and becomes the first in a continuing series of Polaroid instant x-ray products. Type 1001 produces a 10 x 12-inch x-ray print in 60 seconds. The Land Roll Film Back adapts professional cameras and various types of industrial and scientific instruments for use with Polaroid roll films.

1952 Polaroid introduces the Model 110 land camera, called the Pathfinder. This camera is designed for professional use and is equipped with an *f*/4.5 lens and provides shutter speeds to 1/400 of a second.

1953 Polaroid begins to develop x-ray film for the civilian market.

1954 The Model 100 debuts. It features special long-life roller bearings and a heavy-duty shutter. The camera is for use in business and industrial applications.

1955 PolaPan 200 Land picture rolls are introduced to the public.

1956 The one-millionth camera, a Model 95A, comes off the assembly line in September.

1957 Polaroid markets several new cameras, and the Polaroid Transparency System is introduced.

1958 One-step photography is extended to conventional studio and press cameras. The 50 Series of Land films (Types 52 and 53) and the 4 x 5 film holder become almost indispensable proofing tools for the professional photographer.

1959 Polaroid markets the Wink Light Model 250 and Model 252. Type 47 Land film, rated at 3000 ASA, becomes the fastest film available.

1960 Polaroid introduces its first automatic exposure camera: Model 900 with Electronic Eye.

1961 Polaroid releases two electric-eye cameras, the Model J66 and Model J33 in the $75 to $100 range. Type 55 P/N Land film is introduced. Polaroid continues to commission artists as consultants during the early 1960s.

1962 The Polaroid MP-3 Land camera is introduced.

1963 Polaroid debuts Polacolor. Products released this year include the CU-5 Closeup camera, type 510 Land film, featuring high-contrast reproduction for industrial applications and Type 413 Infrared Land film for use in laser research, military surveillance, and document analysis. The 5 millionth Polaroid Land camera, an Automatic 100, comes off the assembly line in Little Rock, Arkansas.

1965 The inexpensive Polaroid Swinger is introduced.

1966 CU-5 closeup framing kits are introduced to the industry. The ID-2 Land Identification System premieres. The ID-2 is the first in a series of self-contained identification systems using Polaroid instant photography. Among its applications, the system will be used for driver's license photos.

1967 Five Electric-eye 200 Series cameras are introduced worldwide. Type 51 film is marketed for high-contrast reproduction of line art work. Speed of Type 1461 Land film is increased to 320 under daylight/electronic flash illumination, 125 under tungsten. Polaroid releases an Instant Halftone System for the MP-3 camera.

1968 Polaroid introduces a number of additional new products: the M-10 camera, for low-level aerial reconnaissance pictures; the Special Events Land camera Model 228, for producing pictures on a high-volume, continuous basis; a new Polaroid 4 X 5 film holder (Model 545).

1969 The Polaroid Model ED-10 Land Instrument camera is introduced for educational institutions and research labs. A special adapter enables it to fit over the eyepiece of a microscope to provide a simple method of making photomicrographs. The Polaroid 300 Series pack cameras are introduced. The top-of the-line Model 360 Land camera represents the first incorporation of integrated circuits into a consumer product and includes an electronic flash.

1970 Coaterless black-and-white film Type 20C for the Swinger camera goes on sale.

1971 The ID-3 Land Identification System is introduced.

1972 The revolutionary SX-70 system realizes Dr. Land's concept of absolute one-step photography: new concepts in camera and film interaction lead to the design of the first fully automatic, motorized folding single lens reflex camera that ejects self-developing, self-timing colour prints.

1973 The Clarence Kennedy Gallery is established. The gallery serves as a showcase for the work of emerging and professional photographers using Polaroid products. The MP-4 technical camera replaces the older MP-3.

1974 Polaroid estimates that well over a billion instant prints will be made this year, about 65% of them being made in colour.

1975 Polaroid begins marketing Polacolor 2 film (Type 108). It is the first peel-apart colour film that uses a colour negative manufactured by Polaroid (Polaroid has made colour negatives for integral X-70 film since its introduction in 1972).

1976 The inexpensive Pronto! camera is introduced. The Pronto! uses SX-70 film and features a distance scale on the lens ring and an automatic electronic exposure setting.

1977 The OneStep Land camera is introduced. Polaroid introduces the 20 x 24-inch camera; the prototype camera weighs 800 pounds. The camera produces colour 20 X 24 inch photographs in 60 seconds. By the 1980s improvements to the camera reduce its weight to 200 pounds and add swings, tilts, and rising fronts.

1978 Research into sonar technology, initiated in 1963, results in the Sonar Autofocus system for the SX-70 and Pronto! cameras. Polavision, a new instant colour motion picture system, makes 2-1/2-minute films in self-developing cassettes. The system includes a camera, a self-developing film called Phototape, and a player.

1979 Polaroid Type 611 video image recording film is introduced for use with medical diagnostic systems. Dr. Land demonstrates Time-Zero film. It is a brilliantly coloured film for the SX-70 that produces an image visible in seconds and a developed print in 1-1/2 minutes.

1980 The Polapulse P100 battery, first developed for SX70 film, is introduced for commercial applications. New products include Polaroid Colorgraph film Type 891, the Polaprinter, and a new 4 X 5 professional pack film system.

1981 The Polaroid Sun System brings the domain of automatic light mixing to amateur picture taking. Polaroid Colorgraph 8 x 10 Land film (Type 891) becomes the first instant colour transparency film for overhead projection. Polaroid also releases a new 4 x 5 eight-exposure pack film system, which includes the Model 550 4 X 5 film holder, PolaPan Type 552 black-and-white film and Polacolor 2 Type 558 colour film.

1982 Ultrasonic Ranging Systems are introduced. They are used in areas from instrumentation testing and hospital use to robotics. The company also introduces the SLR 680, a folding single lens reflex camera using 600 ASA instant colour film. The camera has a built-in strobe that uses sonar to precisely determine the distance to the subject.

1983 The introduction of the 35-mm Autoprocess System makes Polaroid's instant photography products compatible with standard 35-mm cameras and equipment. Autoprocess produces rapid-access colour or black-and-white transparencies without the use of a darkroom. Polaroid enters the computer and video industries. Supercolor video cassettes are premiered abroad with plans for national distribution in 1984. Polaroid introduces Palette, a low-cost computer image recorder that is supplied with Polaroid graphics software.

1984 Technical improvements in existing cameras lead to the Sun 660 Autofocus and Sun 600 LMS. Both include integrated circuitry called SPARR (Strobe Preferred Automatic Rapid Recharge), which allows one to take pictures in rapid succession without recharging the strobe.

1985 Recent developments result in the perfection of a continuous embossing process that makes low-cost, massproduced holograms for commercial applications. The company announces the Polaform Process, a new custom service for the creation and mass production of embossed surface relief holograms, which can be viewed in ordinary light. The first conventional colour transparency films, Polaroid Professional Chrome films, are distributed on a limited basis for commercial and industrial photographers.

1986 The Spectra camera debuts at Jordan Marsh department store in Boston, thirty-eight years after the Polaroid Land camera Model 95 was introduced.

1987 PolaBlue 35-mm instant slide film produces white on-blue images from text, line art, graphs, and charts. A four-minute processing time in a Polaroid processor yields a high quality presentation slide.

1989 The Polaroid 600 series camera is restyled and called Impulse. A conventional, non-instant photographic film called OneFilm is introduced.

1990 Polaroid expands its range of computer peripherals with photographic scanners and computer colour image recorders for PCs and Macintosh environments.

1991 A new Spectra film having high definition becomes available.

1992 Introduction in Europe of a new format film and compact instant camera called Vision.

1993 The Vision camera becomes available in North America. Introduction of a professional rugged camera called ProCam for use in high volume photographic documentation of events occurring in difficult work areas such as construction sites. Polacolor Pro 100, a peel-apart high definition colour film, based on hybrid chemistry becomes available.

3 Units, weights and measures

3.1 Weights and measures

Two systems of weights and measures are still used in the world. (1) The Système Internationale (SI), usually called the *metric system*, is almost universally employed, the exception being in the United States. It originated in France, after the French Revolution, and was intended to be based exclusively on physical quantities available everywhere. It is often called the *cgs system* standing for centimetre, gram, second. (2) The U.S. customary system is symbolized by *fps*, coming from foot, pound, second. These ancient units are based primarily on tradition.

In the United States, the use of the SI is voluntary and is gradually being adopted, especially in scientific and technological contexts. It is used in many photographic applications, such as film sizes (as in 35-mm film), lens focal lengths, and processing formula specifications.

FUNDAMENTAL SI UNITS There are seven SI base units and two supplementary units (numbers 8 and 9 below) from which all other quantities are derived.

1. The *metre*, the unit of length, was originally based on a fraction of the earth's circumference, but inaccurate measurements in the eighteenth century caused an error in the result. Later, the standard was a distance marked on a metal bar kept at the International Bureau of Weights and Measurements near Paris. Now, the definition of the metre is 1,650,763 wavelengths of a specified line in the spectrum of the element krypton-86.
2. The *kilogram* is the unit of mass (approximately, weight). It is based on a cylinder of metal kept at the International Bureau.
3. The second is the unit of time, formerly 1/86,000 part of the mean solar day. Because of variations in the length of the day, the second is now defined as the time required for 9,192,631,770 vibrations associated with the spectrum of the cesium-132 atom.
4. The *kelvin*, the unit of temperature, is equal to 1/100 part of the interval on the Celsius (formerly, centigrade) scale between the freezing point and the boiling point of pure water under standard conditions. One kelvin is equal to 1°C, but zero on the Kelvin scale corresponds to –273°C.
5. The *candela* (formerly, candle), a measure of the intensity of light from a source. It is defined as 1/60 part of the intensity of an ideal blackbody radiator having an area of 1 cm^2 held at the temperature of the freezing point of platinum.
6. The *mole* is a measure of the amount of pure substance that is equal to its molecular weight in grams. This measure is often used in specifying the amounts of concentrations of chemicals.

7. The *ampere* is a measure of electrical current.
8. The *radian*, a measure of plane angle, defined as that angle subtended at the centre of a circle by an arc equal in length to the radius of the circle.
9. The *steradian*, which is the solid angle at the centre of a sphere subtended by a surface area equal to the radius squared.

Hundreds of other units are derived from these nine units. Derived from the candela, for example, are:

1. The *lumen*, the measure of flux, i.e., the flow of light. One lumen is equal to the light passing through a specified solid angle and originating from a light source having an intensity of 1 candela.
2. The *lux*, a measure of illuminance, the light received by $1 m^2$ of surface when the flux is 1 lumen.

PREFIXES In the metric system (SI), prefixes are used to indicate units larger and smaller than the basic ones.

Prefixes for Basic Metric Units

Prefix	Power of 10	Equivalent
tera-	10^{12}	Trillion
giga-	10^{9}	Billion
mega-	10^{6}	Million
kilo-	10^{3}	Thousand
hecta-	10^{2}	Hundred
deka-	10^{1}	Ten
deci-	10^{-1}	One-tenth
centi-	10^{-2}	One-hundredth
milli-	10^{-3}	One-thousandth
micro-	10^{-6}	One-millionth
nano-	10^{-9}	One-billionth
pico-	10^{-12}	One-trillionth

CONVERSIONS

Inches × 25.4 = millimetres (mm)
Feet × 0.305 = metres (m)
U.S. Quarts × 0.9464 = litres
U.S.Gallons × 3.7853 = litres
U.S. Ounces (fluid) × 29.6 = millilitres (ml)
U.S. Ounces (weight) × 28.4 = grams (g)
U.K. Ounces (fluid) × 28.6 = millilitres (ml)
U.K. Pints × 0.568 = litres
U.K. gallon × 4.546 = litres
Pounds × 0.454 = kilograms (kg).
(Fahrenheit temperature –32) × 5/9 = Celsius (centigrade) temperature (°C).
(Celsius temperature × 9/5) + 32 = Fahrenheit temperature
Angular degrees ÷57.3 = radians.

3.2 Units of Measure

The French introduced the metric system in 1789. It was legalized in the United States in 1966 but has yet, except for scientific and technical usage, to gain wide acceptance. The United States is the only industralized country using English units of measure. Scientists world-wide, including American scientists, now use the ISO Standards codified in 1981. Metric units of measure are known as SI units, after the French, Systéme Internationale.

SI Units

Quantity	Unit	Symbol
length	metre	m
mass	kilogram	kg
time	second	s
electric current	ampere	A
thermodynamic temperature	kelvin	K
amount of substance	mole	mol
luminous intensity	candela	cd
plane angle	radian	rad
solid angle	steradian	sr

SI Decimal Prefixes

Value and Equivalent	Unit	Symbol
1 000 000 000 000 000 000 = 10^{16}	exa-	E
1 000 000 000 000 000 = 10^{15}	peta-	P
1 000 000 000 000 = 10^{12}	tera-	T
1 000 000 000 = 10^{9}	giga-	G
1 000 000 = 10^{6}	mega-	M
1 000 = 10^{3}	kilo-	K
100 = 10^{2}	*hecto-	h
10 = 10^{1}	*deka- or deca-	da
1 = 10^{0}	(no prefix)	–
0.1 = 10^{-1}	*deci-	d
0.01 = 10^{-2}	centi	c
0.001 = 10^{-3}	milli-	m
0.000 001 = 10^{-6}	micro-	μ
0.000 000 001 = 10^{-9}	nano-	n
0.000 000 000 001 = 10^{-12}	pico-	p
0.000 000 000 000 001 = 10^{-15}	femto-	f
0.000 000 000 000 000 001 = 10^{-18}	atto-	a

*to be avoided in technical use

Metric Units (rounded off)

Prefix	Metric Unit	U.S. Equivalent						
milli-	= 1/1000	1 millimetre	=	0.039 inch				
centi-	= 1/100	1 centimetre	=	0.39 inch				
deci-	= 1/10	1 decimetre	=	3.937 inches	=	0.32 foot		
		1 metre	=	39.37 inches	=	3.2 feet	=	1.1 yard
deka-	= 10	1 dekametre	=	393.7 inches	=	32 feet	=	11 yards
hecto-	= 100	1 hectometre	=	3397 inches	=	328 feet	=	109 yards
kilo-	= 1000	1 kilometre	=	39300 inches	=	3280 feet	=	1090 yards

3.3 Logarithmic Notations and Arithmetic Equivalents

Log Notations			Arithmetic Notations	
Standard Logs	Photographic Logs	Negative Logs	Decimal Equivalents	Fractional Equivalents
6.60–10	$\bar{4}$.60	–3.40	.0004	4/10,000
6.70–10	$\underline{4}$.70	–3.30	.0005	5/10,000
6.80–10	$\underline{4}$.80	–3.20	.0006	6/10,000
6.90–10	$\underline{4}$.90	–3.10	.0008	8/10,000
7.00–10	$\underline{3}$.00	–3.00	.0010	10/10,000
7.10–10	$\underline{3}$.10	–2.90	.0012	12/10,000
7.20–10	$\underline{3}$.20	–2.80	.0016	16/10,000
7.30–10	$\underline{3}$.30	–2.70	.0020	20/10,000
7.40–10	$\underline{3}$.40	–2.60	.0025	25/10,000
7.50–10	$\underline{3}$.50	–2.50	.0032	32/10,000
7.60–10	$\underline{3}$.60	–2.40	.0040	40/10,000
7.70–10	$\underline{3}$.70	–2.30	.0050	50/10,000
7.80–10	$\underline{3}$.80	–2.20	.0063	63/10,000
7.90–10	$\underline{3}$.90	–2.10	.0080	80/10,000
8.00–10	$\underline{2}$.00	–2.00	.010	10/1,000
8.10–10	$\underline{2}$.10	–1.90	.012	12/1,000
8.20–10	$\underline{2}$.20	–1.80	.016	16/1,000
8.30–10	$\underline{2}$.30	–1.70	.020	20/1,000
8.40–10	$\underline{2}$.40	–1.60	.0.25	25/1,000
8.50–10	$\underline{2}$.50	–1.50	.0.32	32/1,000
8.60–10	$\underline{2}$.60	–1.40	.040	40/1,000
8.70–10	$\underline{2}$.70	–1.30	.050	50/1,000
8.80–10	$\underline{2}$.80	–1.20	.063	63/1,000
8.90–10	$\underline{2}$.90	–1.10	.080	80/1,000
9.00–10	$\underline{1}$.00	–1.00	.10	10/100
9.10–10	$\underline{1}$.10	–0.90	.12	12/100
9.20–10	$\underline{1}$.20	–0.80	.16	16/100
9.30–10	$\underline{1}$.30	–0.70	.20	20/100
9.40–10	$\underline{1}$.40	–0.60	.25	25/100
9.50–10	$\underline{1}$.50	–0.50	.32	32/100
9.60–10	$\underline{1}$.60	–0.40	.40	40/100
9.70–10	$\underline{1}$.70	–0.30	.50	50/100
9.80–10	$\underline{1}$.80	–0.20	.63	63/100
9.90–10	1.90	–0.10	.80	80/100
10.00–10	0.00	0.00	1.00	1/1
10.10–10	0.10		1.2	
10.20–10	0.20		1.6	
10.30–10	0.30		2.0	
10.40–10	0.40		2.5	
10.50–10	0.50		3.2	
10.60–10	0.60		4.0	
10.70–10	0.70		5.0	
10.80–10	0.80		6.3	
10.90–10	0.90		8.0	
11.00–10	1.00		10	
11.10–10	1.10		12	

Log Notations			Arithmetic Notations	
Standard Logs	Photographic Logs	Negative Logs	Decimal Equivalents	Fractional Equivalents
11.20–10	1.20		16	
11.30–10	1.30		20	
11.40–10	1.40		25	
11.50–10	1.50		32	
11.60–10	1.60		40	
11.70–10	1.70		50	
11.80–10	1.80		63	
11.90–10	1.90		80	
12.00–10	2.00		100	
12.10–10	2.10		120	
12.20–10	2.20		160	
12.30–10	2.30		200	

A common range of logarithm values used in photography with the log values expressed in standard form, photographic form, and negative form. The equivalent arithmetic values are given in both decimal and fractional forms for numbers smaller than 1.0.

3.4 Temperature Conversion Scale

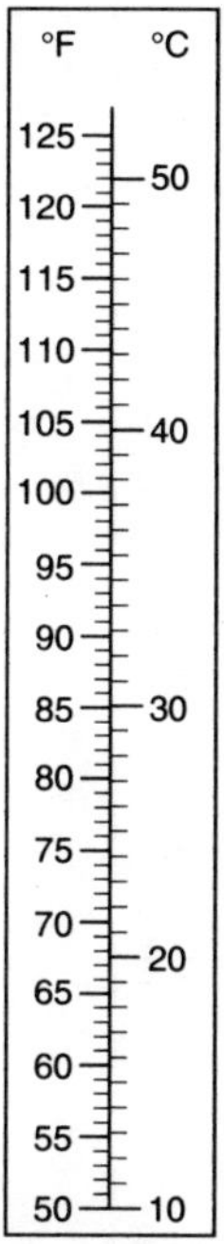

Temperature Conversion Scale

0°C = 32°F   0°F = −17.8°C

0°C = 273 K

Formulas for converting from °C to °F, from °F to °C, from °C to K.

°C = (°F−32) × 5/9   °F = (°C × 9/5) + 32   K = °C + 273

3.5 Distance Conversion Tables

		Metric			U.S.		
		Millimetres mm	Centimetres cm	Metres m	Inches in	Feet ft	Yards yd
Millimetres	mm	1	10	1000	25.4	304.8	914.4
Centimetres	cm	.10	1	100	2.54	30.48	91.44
Metres	m	.001	.01	1	.254	.3048	.9144
Inches	in	.0394	.394	39.37	1	12	36
Feet	ft	.0033	.0328	3.28	.0833	1	3
Yards	yd	.0011	.0109	1.094	.0278	0.333	1

(1Å = 10^{-9} mm ot 20^{-8} cm)

Metric to U.S.			U.S. to Metric		
millimetres	×	0.04 = inches	inches	×	25.4 = millimetres
centimetres	×	0.39 = inches	inches	×	2.54 = centimetres
metres	×	3.28 = feet	feet	×	3.04 = metres
metres	×	1.09 = yards	yards	×	0.91 = metres
kilometres	×	0.62 = miles	miles	×	1.61 kilometres

(kilometres × 5/8 = miles)

Graphic Arts
1 inch = 6 picas
1 pica = 1/6th inch: (.167 inches)

3.6 Area Conversion Tables

Area Measure

U.S. Customary	Metric
square inch (0.007 sq. ft.)	6.452 square centimetres (cm^2) 645.16 square millimetres (mm^2)
square foot (144 sq. in.)	929.03 square centimetres (cm^2) 0.092903 square metre (m^2)
square yard (9 sq. ft.)	0.83613 square metre (m^2)
square rod (30.25 sq. yd.)	
square mile (64 acres)	2.59 square kilometres (km^2)

Metric	U.S. Customary
square millimetre (mm^2)	0.00155 square inch (sq. in.)
square centimetre (cm^2)	0.155 square inch (sq. in.)
square metre	10.764 square feet (sq. ft.,)
square kilometre (km^2)	0.38608 square mile (sq;. mi.)

Metric to U.S.		
square centimetres	× 0.16	= square inches
square metres	× 1.2	= square yards
square kilometres	× 0.4	= square miles

U.S. Metric		
square inches	× 6.5	= square centimetres
square feet	× 0.09	= square metres
square yards	× 0.8	= square metres
square miles	× 2.6	= square kilometres

3.7 Weight and Liquid Measures Conversion Tables

U.S. Customary and Metric Weight Measure

Pounds	Ounces	Grains	Grams	Kilograms
1	16	7000	453.6	0.4536
0.0625	1	437.5	28.35	0.02835
		1	0.0648	
	0.03527	15.43	1	0.001
2.205	35.27	15430	1000	1

U.S. Customary and Metric Liquid Measure

Gallons	Quarts	Fluid ounces	Drams (Fluid)	Millilitres	Litres
1	4	128	1024	3785	3.785
0.25	1	32	256	946.3	0.9463
		1	8	29.57	0.02957
		0.125	1 (60 mins.)	3.697	0.003697
0.2642	1.057	33.81	270.5	1000	1

Conversion Factors

Grains per 32 fluid ounces	×	0.6847	=	grams per litre
Ounces per 32 fluid ounces	×	29.96	=	grams per litre
Pounds per 32 fluid ounces	×	479.3	=	grams per litre
Grams per litre	×	14.60	=	grains per 32 fluid ounces
Grams per litre	×	0.03338	=	ounces per 32 fluid ounces
Grams per litre	×	0.002086	=	pounds per 32 fluid ounces

3.8 Graphical Formula for Diluting Solutions

A Simple Formula for Diluting Solutions

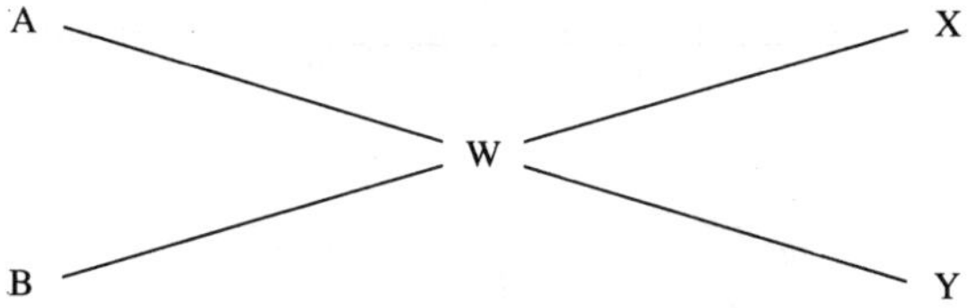

An easy method of figuring dilutions is by the criss-cross method. Place at A the percentage strength of the solution to be diluted and at B the percentage strength of the solution you wish to dilute with (in the case of water, this will be 0). Place at W the percentage strength desired. Now subtract W from A and place at Y. Also subtract B from W and place at X. If you take X parts of A and Y parts of B and mix, you will have a solution of the desired strength W.

For example:
To dilute 99% Acetic Acid to 28%

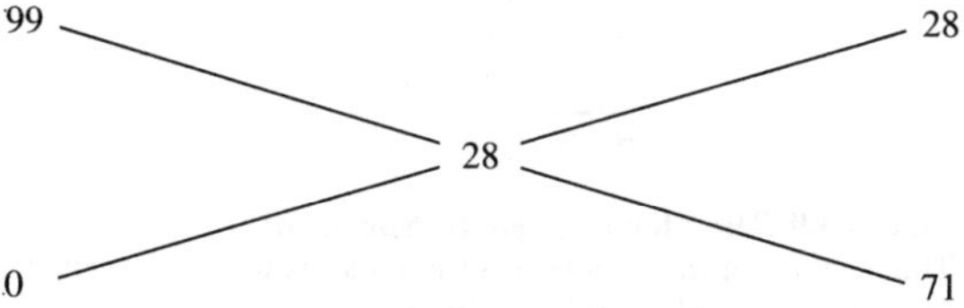

Take 28 parts of 99% Acid and 71 parts water.

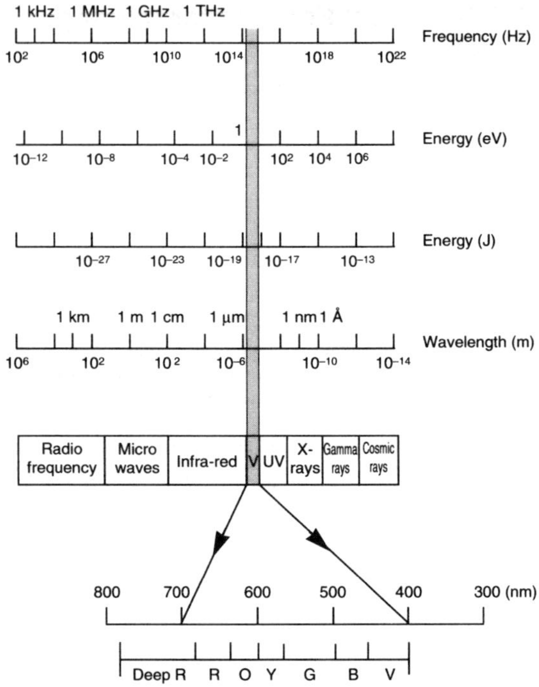

Figure 3.9 The Electromagnetic Spectrum
The position of the visible spectrum and its properties relative to other regions of the full spectrum.

Table 3.10 Spectral line wavelengths (Fraunhofer Lines) used to determine refractive index.

Designation	Wavelength	Element	Line colour
h	404.66	Hg	Violet
g	435.83	Hg	Blue
F′	479.99	Cd	Blue
F	486.13	H	Blue
e	546.07	Hg	Green
d	587.07	Hg	Green
C′	643.85	Cd	Red
C	656.27	H	Red
r	706.52	He	Red

4 Photographic materials

4.1 Image formats

Table 4.1.1 Film formats in photography

Film type, designation or width	Nominal format sizes (mm)
Disc	8 × 10
9.5 mm wide (Minox)	8 × 11
16 mm wide (unperforated)	13 × 17 11.75 × 16.5, 23.5 × 16.5, 10 × 12.5, 20 × 12.5 (microfiche)
35 mm (unperforated)	28 × 40 (828), 28 × 28 (126) 28.30 × 40, 28.30 × 20.00, 28.00 × 14.5 (microfilm)
35 mm wide (perforated) (135)	24 × 18 (half-frame), 24 × 23 (Robot, stereo) 24 × 32, 24 × 36, 24 × 56 (panoramic), 12 × 36 (panoramic)
45mm wide (unperforated) (127)	30 × 40, 40 × 40, 40 × 65
62 mm wide (unperforated) (120/220/620)	60 × 45, 60 × 60 (2¼ inch square), 60 × 70 (ideal format), 60 × 80, 60 × 90, 28 × 40 (24 on 120), 60 × 120, 60 × 170, 60 × 240
70 mm wide (perforated)	40 × 40 (superslide), 60 × 120, 60 × 170, 57 × 239 (panoramic aerial)
Self-developing film	67 × 90, 78 × 78, 90 × 120, 54 × 73
127 mm wide (unperforated)	114 × 886, 114 × 505, 114 × 970 (panoramic)
241 mm wide (unperforated)	230 × 230 (aerial)
Sheet film	65 × 90, 90 × 120, 130 × 180, 180 × 240. Imperial sizes in inches: 2¼ × 3¼, 2½ × 3½, 3¼ × 4¼ (quarter-plate), 3½ × 5½ (postcard), 4 × 5, 4¾ × 6½ (half-plate), 6½ × 8½ (whole plate), 8 × 10, 11 × 14

Table 4.1.2 Cine camera formats

Perforated film width	Name	Camera aperture or film gate dimensions (height × width, mm)
35 mm	Academy	21.95 × 16.00
	Anamorphic	21.95 × 18.59
	Full frame	24.89 × 18.67
	Techniscope	22.05 × 9.47
16 mm	Standard 16	10.26 × 7.49
	Super 16	12.40 × 7.49
16 mm (double run)	Standard 8	4.80 × 3.51
9.5 mm	—	8.5 × 6.5
8 mm	Super 8	6.22 × 4.22

Table 4.1.3 Video and CCD sensor formats

Nominal tube diameter (mm (in))	Scanned image dimensions (height × width, mm)	Image diagonal (mm)
13(½)	4.8 × 6.4	8
17(⅔)	6.6 × 8.8	11
25(1)	9.6 × 12.8	16
30 (1⅓)	12.84 × 17.12	21
3 inch image orthicon (obsolete)	27.43 × 36.58	46
Sensor size (mm)	**Number of pixels (H × V (total))**	**Nominal size (mm (in))**
4.8 × 3.6	768 × 494 (380k)	8.5(⅓)
6.5 × 4.85	752 × 582 (438k) (PAL 625, 8.6 × 8.3μm)	12(½)
	610 × 492 (251k)	
8.8 × 6.6	768 × 494 (380k)	17(⅔)
	510 × 492 (251k)	
11.9 × 8.9	768 × 494 (380k)	25(1)
61.44 × 61.44 (Megapixel)	5120 × 5120 (26.2M) (12 × 12) μm	
	4096 × 4096 (16.8M)	
	3072 × 2048 (6.3M)	

4.1.4 Video sensor formats

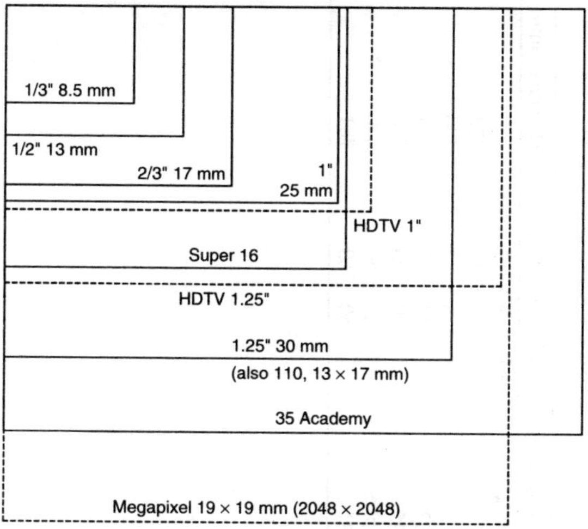

Included are proposed HDTV formats and, for comparison, 16 and 35 mm cine formats and the 110 Pocket Instamatic format.

Table 4.1.5 Copy and format sizes in process camera work

Format	Size(mm)	Diagonal (mm)	Format (inch)	Diagonal (inch)	Format (cm)	Diagonal (mm)
DIN A0	841 × 1189	1456	4 × 5	6.4	9 × 12	150
DIN A1	594 × 841	1030	5 × 7	8.6	13 × 18	222
DIN A2	420 × 594	728	11 × 14	17.8	18 × 24	300
DIN A3	297 × 420	514	14 × 17	22	24 × 20	384
DIN A4	210 × 297	364	16 × 20	25.6	30 × 40	500
DIN A5	148 × 210	257	17 × 23	28.6	40 × 50	640
DIN A6	105 × 148	182	20 × 24	31.2	50 × 60	781

Table 4.1.6 Diapositive projection formats.

Nominal format (mm)	Slide mount aperture dimensions (mm)	Area (mm^2)	Diagonal (mm)
12 × 18	12 × 17	204	20.8
13 × 17	12 × 16	192	20
18 × 24	17 × 23	391	28.6
24 × 24	23 × 23	529	32.5
28.1 × 28.6	26 × 26	676	36.7
24 × 36	23 × 35	805	41.8
24 × 36	23.4 × 34.8*	814	41.9
24 × 36	23.4 × 31.1†	728	38.9
40 × 40	37.3 × 37.3	1444	53.7
60 × 60	54 × 54	2916	76.4
60 × 70	55 × 70	3850	89
85 × 85	73 × 73	5329	103.2
85 × 100	73 × 88	6424	114.3
255 × 255	255 × 255‡	65025	361

*for accurate pin registration
†TV and 16 mm cine format aspect ratio of 3 : 4
‡overhead projector

Table 4.1.7 Cine projection formats

Type	Aspect ratio	Gate dimensions (mm)	Area (mm^2)	Diagonal (mm)
Standard 8 mm	1 : 1.33	3.3 × 4.4	14.5	5.5
Super 8 mm	1 : 1.34	4.0 × 5.35	21.4	6.7
16 mm	1 : 1.34	7.16 × 9.60	69	12.0
35 mm	1 : 1.37	15.2 × 20.90	318	25.8
35 mm	1 : 1.66	12.57 × 20.90	262	24.6
35 mm	1 : 1.75	11.94 × 20.90	248	24.1
35 mm	1 : 1.85	11.30 × 20.90	236	23.7
Cinemascope (magnetic sound)	1 : 2.55	18.16 × 23.16	420	29.5
Cinemascope (optical sound)	1 : 2.35	18.16 × 21.30	386	28.0
Todd AO 70 mm	1: 2.21	22.0 × 48.59	1065	53.0

4.1.8 Slide Mount Sizes and Formats

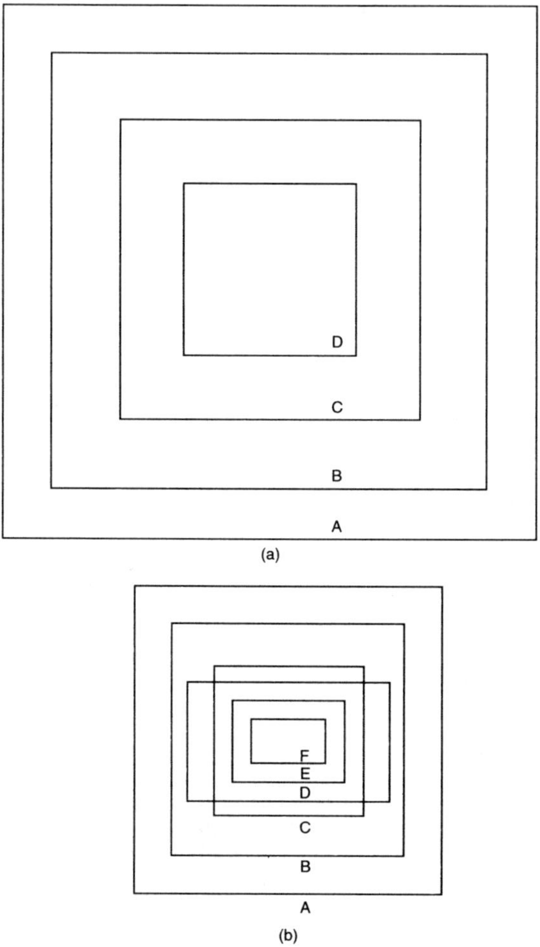

(a) Relative sizes of four slide mounts in common use: A, 82.5 × 82.5mm (3¼ × 3¼ inch). B, 70 × 70 mm. C, 50 × 50 mm (2 × 2 inch). D, 30 × 30 mm. (b) A selection of transparency formats used in the 50 × 50 mm mount (A). B, 40 × 40 mm. C, 28 × 28 mm. D, 24 × 36 mm. E, 18 × 24 mm. f, 13 × 17 mm.

4.2.1 Agfa Film Reciprocity Data

Agfapan APX 25

Reciprocity effect

Measured exposure time (s)	1/1000 to ½	1	10	100
Exposure correction (lens stops)	none	+1	+1½	+2
Development correction (%)	none	none	none	none

Agfapan APX 100

Reciprocity effect

Measured exposure time(s)	1/1000 to ½	1	10	100
Exposure correction (lens stops)	none	+1	+2	+3
Development correction (%)	none	−10	−25	−35

To obtain the same contrast range the developing time must be shortened.

Agfapan APX 400

Reciprocity effect

Measured exposure time (s)	1/1000 to ½	1	10	100
Exposure correction (lens stops)	none	+1	+2½	+3½
Development correction (%)	none	−10	−25	−35

To obtain the same contrast range the developing time must be shortened.

Agfaortho 25

Reciprocity effect

Measured exposure time(s)	1/1000 to ½	1	10	100
Exposure correction (lens stops)	none	none	+⅔	+1⅓

Agfa Dia Direct

Reciprocity effect

Measured exposure time(s)	1/10000	−10	100
Exposure correction (lens stops)	none		+½

(Courtesy Agfa)

4.2.2 Fuji Film Reciprocity Data

Reciprocity Data for Neopan 400 and Neopan 1600 Films

Exposure Times	Adjustment
½ second to 1/8,000th of a second	none
1 second	+ ½ stop
10 seconds	+ 1 stop
100 seconds	+ 2 stops

(Courtesy Fuji)

4.2.3 Ilford Film Reciprocity Data

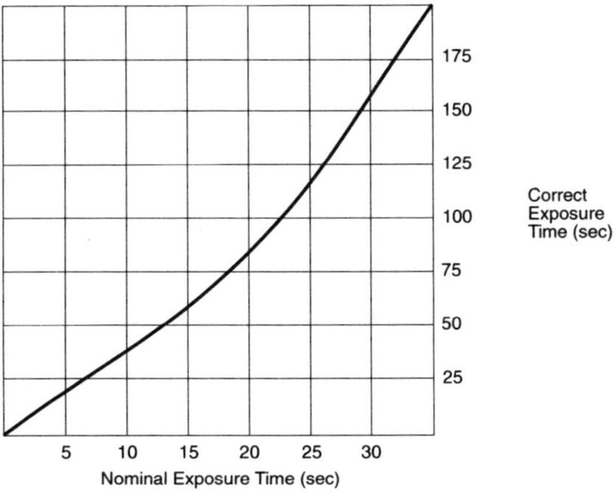

Medium Speed and High Speed

ISO 100 100 Delta
ISO 125 FP4+

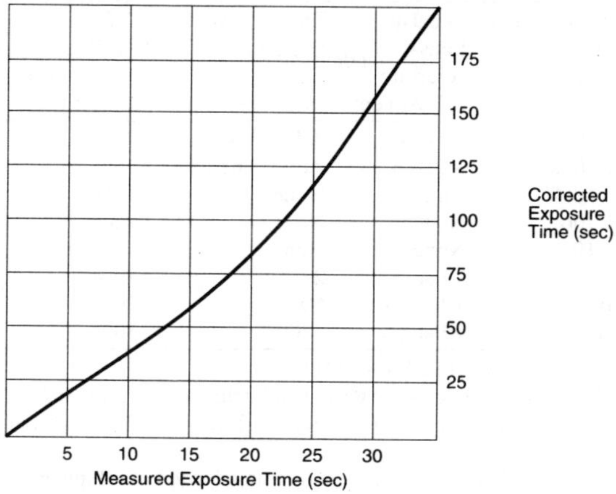

Medium Speed and High Speed

ISO 100 100 Delta
ISO 125 FP4+
ISO 400 400 Delta
ISO 400 HP5+
ISO 400 XP2

(Courtesy Ilford)

4.2.4 Kodak Film Reciprocity Data

Adjustments for long and short exposures

Use the exposure and development adjustments in the table on the following pages for these black-and-white films:

KODAK EKTAPAN Film
KODAK PLUS-X Pan Film
KODAK PLUS-X Pan Professional Film
KODAK ROYAL Pan Film
KODAK SUPER-XX Pan Film
KODAK TRI-X Pan Film
KODAK TRI-X Pan Professional Film

Exposure and Development Adjustments for Most Black-and-White Films

If Calculated Exposure Time is (Seconds)	Use This Lens-Aperture Adjustment *OR*	This Adjusted Exposure Time (Seconds)	AND Use This Development Adjustment
1/100,000*†‡	+1 stop	Adjust aperture	+20%
1/10,000*†‡	+½ stop	Adjust aperture	+15%
1/1000	None	None	+10%§
1/100	None	None	None
1/10	None	None	None
1	+1 stop	2	–10%
10	+2 stops	50	–20%
100	+3 stops	1200	–30%

*Not applicable to EKTAPAN Film
†Not recommended for TRI-X Pan Professional Film/4164
‡Not recommended for ROYAL Pan Film or SUPER-XX Pan film
§EKTAPAN Film does not require an adjusted development time at 1/1000 second.

Exposure and Develpment Adjustments for KODAK Commercial Film

If Calculated Exposure Time is (Seconds)	Use This Lens-Aperture Adjustment *OR*	This Adjusted Exposure Time (Seconds)	AND Use This Development Adjustment
1/100	None	None	+10%
1/25	None	None	None
1/10	None	None	–10%
1	None	None	–20%
10	+½ stop	15	–30%
100	+1 stop	300	–40%

Exposure and Development Adjustments fof KODAK Technical Pan Film (developed in KODAK TECHNIDOL Liquid Developer or KODAK HC-110 Developer [Dil D])

If Calculated Exposure Time is (Seconds)	Use This Lens-Aperture Adjustment *OR*	This Adjusted Exposure Time (Seconds)	AND Use This Development Adjustment
1/10,000	None	None	+30%
1/1000	None	None	+20%
1/100	None	None	None
1/10	None	None	None
1	None	None	–10%
10	+½ stop	15	–10%
100	+1½ stops	NR	None

NR = Not recommended

4.2.5 Kodak T-MAX film

Exposure Adjustments for

If Calculated Exposure Time is (Seconds)	KODAK T-MAX 100 Professional Film: Use This Lens-Aperture Adjustment	OR	KODAK T-MAX 100 Professional Film: This Adjusted Exposure Time (Seconds)	KODAK T-MAX 400 Professional Film: Use This Lens-Aperture Adjustment	OR	KODAK T-MAX 400 Professional Film: This Adjusted Exposure Time (Seconds)	KODAK T-MAX P3200 Professional Film: Use This Lens-Aperture Adjustment	OR	KODAK T-MAX P3200 Professional Film: This Adjusted Exposure Time (Seconds)
1/10,000	+⅓ stop		Adust aperture	None		None	None		None
1/1000	None		None	None		None	None		None
1/100	None		None	None		None	None		None
1/10	None		None	None		None	None		None
1	+⅓ stop		Adjust aperture	+⅓ stop		Adjust aperture	None		None
10	+½ stop		15	+½ stop		15	+⅔ stop		15
100	+1 stop		200	+1 ½ stops		300	+2 stops		400

Note: KODAK T-MAX Professional Films do not require a development-time adjustment.
(Courtesy Eastman Kodak Co.)

4.2.6 Polaroid Film Reciprocity Data

POLAROID TYPE 52 AND TYPE 55

Reciprocity

Indicated Exposure Time	Use Either Adjustment Aperture	or	Exposure Time
1/1000 sec.	None		None
1/100 sec.	None		None
1/10 sec.	None		None
1 sec.	None		None
10 sec.	+⅓ stop		+3 sec.
100 sec.	+1 stop		+100 sec.

POLAROID TYPE 665

Reciprocity

Indicated Exposure Time	Use Either Adjustment Aperture	or	Exposure Time
1/1000 sec.	None		None
1/100 sec.	None		None
1/10 sec.	None		None
1 sec.	None		None
10 sec.	+½ stop		+5 sec.
100 sec.	+1⅓ stops		+150 sec.

(Courtesy Polaroid Corp.)

4.2.7 Ilford Paper Reciprocity Data

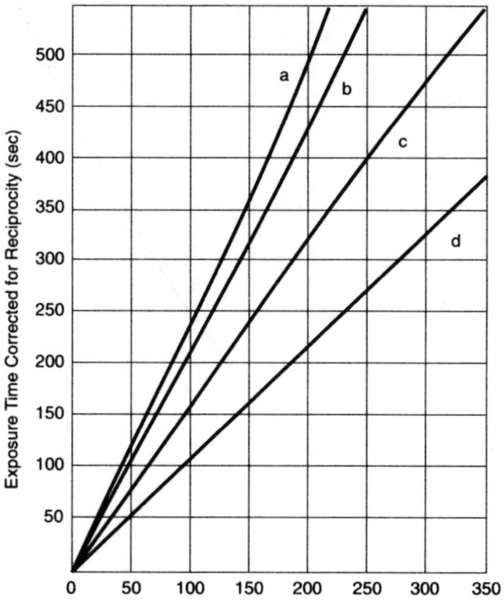

Average Reciprocity Curves for Ilford Enlarging Papers

a) Ilfobrom Galerie FB
b) Ilfospeed RC Deluxe
c) Multigrade FB
d) Multigrade III RC

(Courtesy Ilford)

4.2.8 Kodak Paper Reciprocity Data

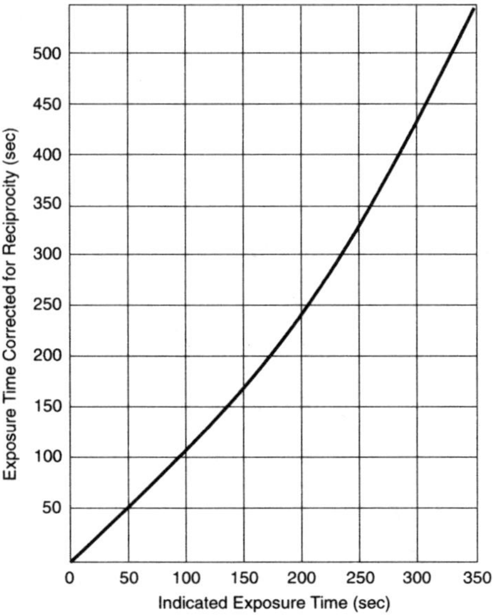

KODAK Reciprocity Curve for Enlarging Papers

All photographic papers and films are affected by reciprocity failure with extended for very short exposure *times*. For printing exposure times of 1 to 4 minutes, increase exposure time about 20 to 30%; for printing exposure times from 4–1/2 to 6 minutes, increase the time to about 40 to 50%. The required increase in time to compensate for reciprocity will vary depending upon the choice of paper.

(Courtesy Eastman Kodak Co.)

4.3.1 Infra-red photography

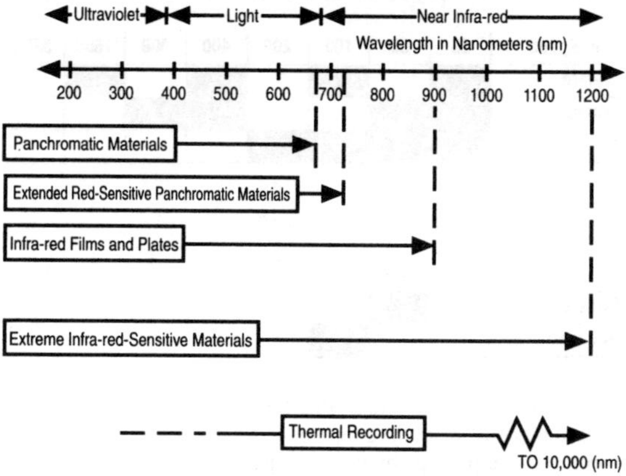

Infra-red photography. The spectral ranges of panchromatic materials, extended red-sensitive panchromatic materials, infra-red films and places, extreme infra-red-sensitive materials, and thermal recording. (Reprinted courtesy of Eastman Kodak Company.)

4.3.2 DX codes

The "DX" pattern of squares on a 35mm cassette was introduced to program the film speed automatically into the camera, and has now been almost universally adopted. The pattern of conductive and insulating squares forms two columns stretching down the cassette from top to bottom. The squares are in three basic groups: the left-hand column (seen with the spool protruding at the bottom of the cassette) controls film speed set; in the right-hand column the second, third and fourth squares specify film length, and the bottom two describe the film type—negative or reversal. The top two squares in each row are always silver.

Few current cameras use all squares, but most newer models make use of the film speed setting squares, and on some cameras there is no manual adjustment of film speed: if your films are over- or underexposed you can't adjust the camera to make a correction. You can, however, adjust the cassette.

Before trying this, though, check the contacts in the camera's cassette compartment. The simplest cameras read only squares 2 and 4, and distinguish between films with speeds of ISO 100, 200, 400 and 800. Cameras with five contacts, to read squares 2—6, set film speeds to within 1/3 stop between ISO 25 and 5000.

To alter the ISO value programmed into one of these cameras, it is necessary to know how the code works. Squares 2, 3 and 4 set the film speed on a doubling basis—25, 50, 100, 200 and so on. Squares 5 and 6 fine-tune exposure by 1/3 stop intervals. When 2, 3 and 4 are all black, ISO 25 is set. When square 2 is silver, it doubles film speed: so when 2 is silver and 3 and 4 black, ISO 50 is set. Similarly, square 3 quadruples film speed and square 4 multiplies it by 16. In combination, the three squares can specify film speed from ISO 25 to 3200, as shown here:

Film Speed	25	50	100	200	400	800	1600	3200
Square 2	■		■		■		■	
Square 3	■	■			■	■		
Square 4	■	■	■	■				

To fine-tune exposure, use the other two squares:

	+¤÷#	+/÷#	+ 0
Square 5		■	
Square 6			■

So, for example, to rate an ISO 50 transparency film at EI 64, stick a piece of insulating tape over square 6 and make square 5 conductive, perhaps by using a square of metal foil.

4.3.3 Batch-testing film

Practical tests enable you to predict how film will perform under real conditions or to compare similar films. Tests should reflect how you work—if you take mainly landscapes, don't test the film using studio flash. This, indeed, is an argument in favour of assessing film yourself rather than relying on published reports.

The following subjects test most of the important characteristics of today's colour films:

Grey scale This need not be a printed scale, but it should include an 18 per cent grey card as a reference tone. Crumpled black fabric provides a good test of shadow detail. Any brilliant white object tests highlight detail and reveals grain structure—flowers are a good choice.

Primary colours Brilliant hues tax the abilities of a film to the extreme, and arguably provide the most noticeable differences between various emulsions. Brightly coloured, yet detailed, subjects, such as clothing, are a better choice than uniform tones, since some films sacrifice detail when colours (especially red) are highly saturated.

Flesh tones Most film manufacturers aim to create neutral or slightly warm skin tones, but achieving this objective may mean sacrificing neutrality of highlights or shadows. So in evaluating transparencies, take care to compare the hues of skin tones with dark and light areas.

Fine detail If possible, incorporate fine detail in all areas of the tonal scale in order to check sharpness in both highlights and shadows. Fur or hair makes a good subject.

White fabric Many white fabrics fluoresce in ultraviolet light, and though the human eye has little sensitivity to the blue colour this creates, some films exaggerate it. White fabric tests for this problem.

Blue flowers At the other end of the spectrum, many blue flowers and some green synthetic fibres reflect strongly in the near infra-red. Again, the eye is insensitive to these wavelengths, but some films do pick them up, turning blue flowers mauve. Corrective filtration is almost impossible, so testing for this characteristic is of fundamental importance in some specialist fields. To check if a subject reflects very deep red, view it through a deep red Wratten 70 filter using tungsten light, and make a comparison with a subject of similar colour that is known to reproduce well on film.

Consistency Take care to match illuminant colour to the film's sensitivity, or use filtration to correct any imbalance. Shoot films to be compared in the same camera and bracket pictures over a wide range at ⅓-stop intervals to check true speed. Most of all, be sure to use photographic techniques that reflect your normal practice: don't, for example, use an incident light meter if your normally rely on the meter built in to the camera.

4.3.4 Film storage before processing

The useful life of film depends not only on how you store it, but also on how critical you are. "Professional" emulsions are manufactured for critical use and are supplied in optimum condition. To maintain this peak of "ripeness", these films must be stored with great care. Films manufactured for amateurs are despatched in "unripe" form and need less-careful storage.

Temperature For long-term storage keep all types of colour film refrigerated— at 10°C (50°F) or colder; professional emulsions should be kept at a lower temperature even in the short term. High temperatures will damage any film, including monochrome emulsions, so avoid sources of heat, such as a flash power pack that may warm up in use or the rear window shelf of a car. Freezing film slows changes in the emulsion and may be worthwhile for extended storage. However, bear in mind that freezing does not slow all sources of change, as explained below. Freezers for storing film should be kept in the range 0° to –10°C (–18° –23°F).

Frozen and refrigerated film needs time to warm to room temperature before the package is opened. Take the film from its outer packing, separate the cartons and stand them on their smallest side, then leave them at room temperature for the times indicated below. Don't hurry the procedure by using heat sources such as a hair dryer.

Warm-up times (hrs/min)

Packing	Temp rise 14°C (57°F)	56°C (132°F)
35mm cassettes	1	1.30
Roll film	0.30	1
25 sheets (any size)	1	1.30
50 sheets	2	3
35mm bulk tin	3	5
70mm, 100ft	3	5

Ionizing radiation The most familiar source of ionizing radiation is the airport X-ray machine, but the natural environment everywhere emits some background radiation that can in time harm film. The effect is worth considering only with ultra-high-speed films and long-term storage: with these films the value of freezing (as opposed to refrigeration) is debatable.

Humidity Damp conditions damage film, and though film packaging inhibits moisture penetration, only foil wraps are hermetically sealed. Ideally, store film in low-humidity conditions —below 60 per cent relative humidity. You can measure humidity using a variety of methods, but common sense also provides important clues—if labels start to curl up, for example, then the humidity is too high.

If your chosen storage place is naturally humid (refrigerators and freezers are), protect film in an airtight container, such as a polythene bag or a screw-topped jar. Note, however, that adhesive tape does not form a watertight seal, so tins sealed with tape are suitable only for the short-term storage of film.

Chemical hazards Many everyday items give off gases that harm films. Solvents and mothballs are particular hazards, but mercury vapour from broken thermometers and exhaust fumes from motor vehicles are perhaps less obvious culprits. All these compounds damage film and they may be given off in small quantities by cleaning compounds, paints and adhesives: even some camera bags emit formaldehyde. Store film away from obvious sources of these hazards, in airtight containers where possible.

Hazardous substances

- Ammonia
- Paints
- Solvents
- Cleaners
- Adhesives
- Chipboard
- Sulphides
- Glue
- Mothballs
- Motor vehicle exhausts
- Permanent-press trousers (!)
- Stain-resistant fabric finishes
- Mildew preventatives
- Insecticides
- Foam in place insulation
- Industrial pollution
- Particle board
- Cavity-wall insulation

Physical factors These hazards are so obvious that they are frequently overlooked. A household catastrophe, such as a leaking pipe, can be doubly damaging if the deluge engulfs 100 rolls of film stored at floor level. Simple precautions are all that's needed to prevent film being crushed, burned, soaked, fumigated, eaten by rats or rendered useless in some other way.

After exposure Whenever possible, film should be processed immediately after exposure. If processing is delayed, follow the same storage guidelines as for unexposed film. Where processing services are unreliable, it may seem more sensible to post film to a distant location for processing. However, this requires careful consideration, because mailbags may sit for hours in a locked van on the hot airport tarmac. In preference, post film at a main sorting office, or if the mail is not reliable, take postage-paid packages to the airport and pass them to passengers on homeward-bound flights.

5 Lens and camera data

Table 5.1 Features of types of lens configurations

Name or type	Basic optical construction	Exceptional for	Poor for	Special features or advantages of this design or construction	Uses
Meniscus	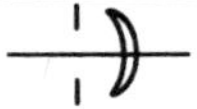		A, D, F	Cheap, low flare	Simple cameras, close-up lenses
Landscape	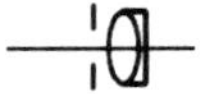	CA	A, F	Achromatic	Simple cameras, close-up lenses
Soft-focus portrait	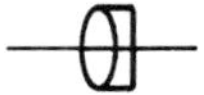		Deliberate spherical aberration	Controllable residual aberration	Portraiture
Petzval	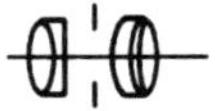	S	A, F	Large aperture, good correction	Portraiture, projection
Symmetrical	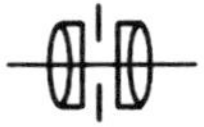	D	F	Distortion-free	General
Double anastigmat	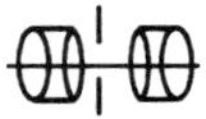	D	S	Distortion-free, components usable separately	General

Table 5.1 continued

Name or type	Basic optical construction	Exceptional for	Poor for	Special features or advantages of this design or construction	Uses
Double Gauss	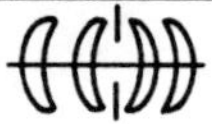	S, C	D	Large apertures possible	Low light level work
Triplet	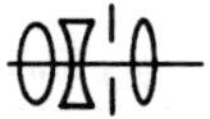			Good correction for all aberrations, cheap	General
Quasi-symmetrical	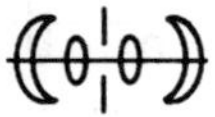	D		Wide-angle lens, distortion-free	Aerial survey work, rangefinder cameras
Process	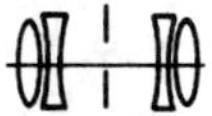	All		Highly corrected	Copying and close-up work
Telephoto	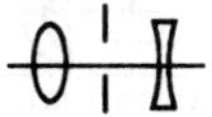		D	Short back focus, compact	Long-focus lens
Retrofocus	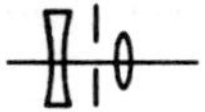		D	Long back focus, reflex focusing	Wide-angle lens for SLR cameras

Table 5.1 continued

Name or type	Basic optical construction	Exceptional for	Poor for	Special features or advantages of this design or construction	Uses
Fisheye	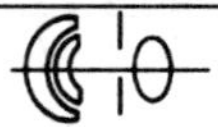		Deliberate distortion	Field angle exceeding 180°, reflex focusing	Cloud studies, special effects
Zoom	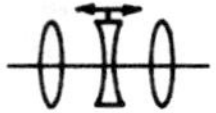		D	Variable focal length with constant *f* number	General
Mirror	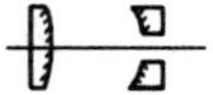	S, CA, L	A, F	Compact construction, lightweight	Long focus lens

S, spherical aberration. CA, chromatic aberration. L, lateral colour. C, coma. A, astigmatism. D, distortion. F, field curvature.

Table 5.2 Lens types and features for 35 mm SLR cameras

Type	Focal length/ range (mm)	Typical maximum f-number	Field of view (diagonal degrees)	Construction	Typical number of elements	Features
Fisheye	6–10	4–2.8	220–180	Extreme retrofocus	7–12	Circular image Filter turret
Quasi-fisheye	10–16	3.5	180–100	Extreme retrofocus	6–10	Frame filled Barrel distortion
Extreme wide-angle	13–18	3.5	120–100	Retrofocus	9–13	Floating element
Very wide-angle	20–24	2.8–2	94–84	Retrofocus	8–10	Close focus Floating element
Wide-angle	28–35	2–1.4	75–62	Double Gauss or retrofocus	6–9	Large aperture
Standard	40–55	1.4–1	56–43	Triplet, Tessar Sonnar, Double Gauss	3–7	Large aperture
Short telephoto	75–105	2.8–1.4	37–23	Double Gauss or telephoto	5	Compact Large aperture
Medium telephoto	120–200	4–2	21–12	Tessar, telephoto	4–6	Internal focusing Large aperture

Table 5.2 continued

Type	Focal length/ range (mm)	Typical maximum f-number	Field of view (diagonal degrees)	Construction	Typical number of elements	Features
Long telephoto	300–500	8–2.8	8–5	Telephoto	4–7	ED glass
Extreme telephoto	600–1200	11–5.6	4–2	Doublet, telephoto	2–5	ED glass
Mirror	250–2000	11–5.6	10–1.3	Catadioptric	5–8	Filter turret
Very wide to wide-angle	21–35	3.5	90–62	Zoom	10	Variable aperture
zoom	24–35	2.8	84–62		9	
Wide angle to standard zoom	24–50	3.5	84–46	Zoom	8–12	Close focus mode
Wide to short tele	35–70	3.5	62–35	Zoom	7–10	
zoom	28–85	2.8	75–29	Varifocal	8–12	
Short to long tele zoom	80–200	4	30–12	Zoom	8–15	Matched multiplier
Extended range zoom	50–300	4.5	46–8	Zoom	15	
Macro	40–200	2.8	60–12	Double Gauss	4–6	Macro focusing
Soft focus	85–100	2.8–2	28–25	Triplet	3–5	
Perspective control	24–35	2.8	75–62	Retrofocus	8–12	Tilt and shift

Table 5.3 Lens types and features for 120 roll film SLR cameras

Type	Focal length/ range (mm)	Typical maximum f-number	Field of view (diagonal degrees)	Construction	Typical number of elements	Features
Quasi-fisheye	24–30	3.5	180	Extreme retrofocus	9–11	
Extreme wide-angle	40	4	90	Retrofocus	10–12	
Very wide-angle	50	2.8	75	Retrofocus	7–10	Floating element
Wide-angle	60	3.5	65	Retrofocus	7	
Standard	75–80	2.8–1.9	56–52	Double Gauss	5–7	Large aperture
Short tele	90–110	3.5–2	48–39	Double Gauss	6	Large aperture
Medium tele	150	4–2.8	30	Sonnar	6	Compact
Long tele	250	5.6	18	Sonnar	5	
Very long tele	350–500	5.6	13–9	Telephoto	5	
Mirror	500–1000	8–5.6	9–4.5	Catadioptric	6	
Macro	120–140	5.6	36–13	Double Gauss	6	Flat field
Medium tele zoom	140–280	5.6	13–6.5	Zoom	17	Close focus mode
Perspective control	75	4.5	50	Retrofocus	9	Shifts
Soft focus	145	4	34	Triplet derivative	7	Spherical aberration

Table 5.4 Focal length, field of view and lens type.

Focal length (mm)	Nominal format (mm)	Angle of view (degrees on diagonal)	Lens type
15	24 × 36	110	EWA
20	24 × 36	94	EWA
24	24 × 36	84	WA
35	24 × 36	63	SWA
40	24 × 36	57	S
40	60 × 60	94	EWA
50	24 × 36	47	S
50	60 × 60	81	WA
50	60 × 70	85	WA
65	24 × 36	37	MLF
65	60 × 60	66	SWA
65	4 × 5 in	103	EWA
80	60 × 60	56	S
90	24 × 36	27	MLF
90	4 × 5 in	84	WA
135	24 × 36	18	LF
135	60 × 60	35	MLF
135	4 × 5 in	62	S
150	60 × 60	32	LF
150	4 × 5 in	57	S
200	24 × 36	12	LF
200	8 × 10 in	78	WA
250	60 × 60	19	LF
300	24 × 36	8	VLF
300	8 × 10 in	57	S
500	24 × 36	5	VLF
500	60 × 60	10	LF
500	4 × 5 in	19	LF
1000	24 × 36	2.5	ELF
1000	60 × 60	5	VLF
1000	4 × 5 in	9	LF
1000	8 × 10 in	19	LF

Abbreviations: EWA, extreme wide-angle; WA, wide-angle; SWA, semi-wide-angle; S, standard; MLF, medium long focus: LF, long focus; VLF, very long focus; ELF, extreme long focus.

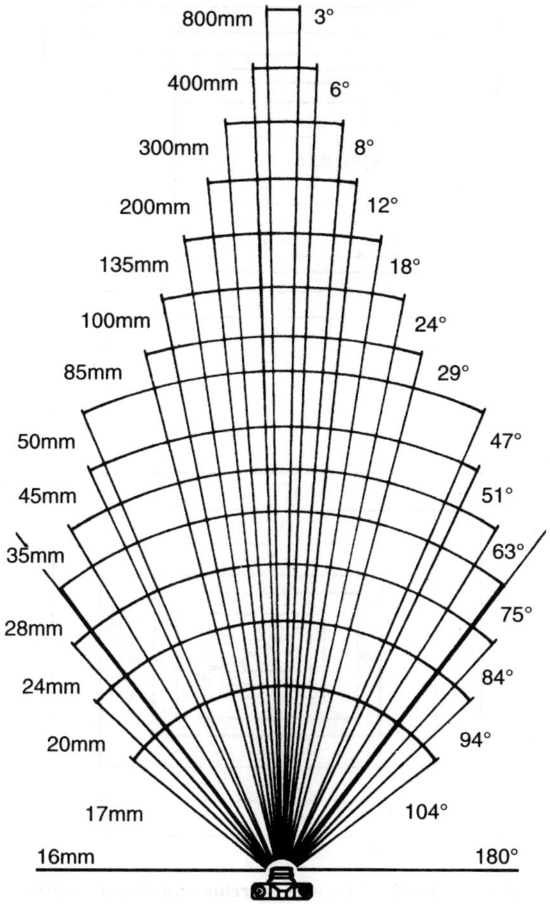

Figure 5.5 Diagonal Field of View of Lenses for the 24 × 36 mm Format

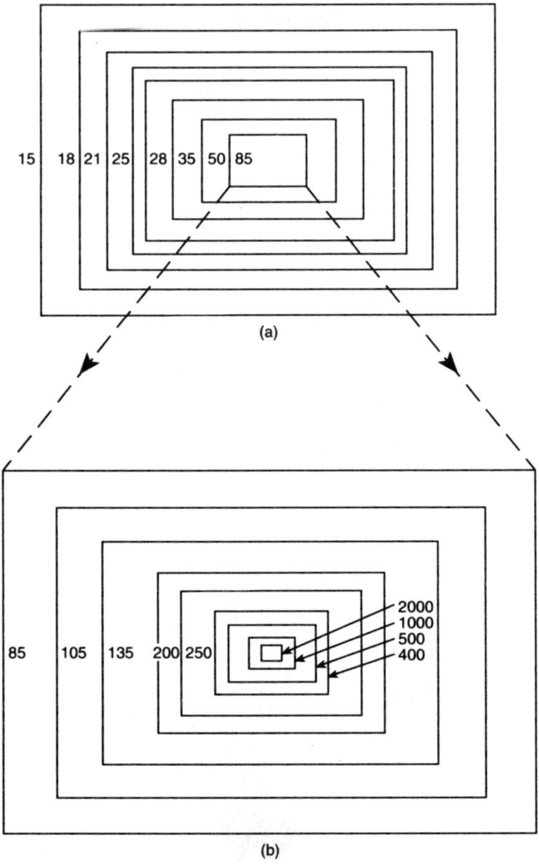

Figure 5.6 Fields of View of Extreme Long Focus Lenses Comparative subject coverage on 24 × 36 mm format for lenses of EFL 15–2000 mm. (a) Extreme wide angle to medium long focus. (b) Medium long-focus to extreme long focus.

Table 5.7 Properties of enlarger lenses

Format (mm)	Focal length (mm)	Field of view (degree)	Maximum aperture (f-no)	Optimum aperture (f-no)	Standard magnification	Magnification range	Number of elements	Design type
18 × 24	28	52	4	8	10	2–20	6	DG
24 × 36	50	52	2.8	5.6	10	2–20	6	A
24 × 36	50	52	2.8	11	10	2–20	4	RT
24 × 36	50	52	2.8	11	4	2–8	3	T
24 × 36	40	60	4	8	10	2–30	6	WA
32 × 45	70	40	4	8	10	5–20	8	A
40 × 40	60	52	4	8	10	2–10	6	DG
60 × 60	80	50	4	8	10	2–20	6	DG
60 × 60	75	52	4.5	11	4	2–6	4	RT
60 × 60	60	60	4	11	10	2–30	6	WA
60 × 70	90	55	5.6	11	6	2–10	6	P
60 × 90	95	47	5.6	11	5	2–10	4	RT
60 × 90	105	51	5.6	11	5	2–10	6	P
60 × 90	105	51	4	8	8	2–15	7	A
90 × 120	135	54	5.6	11	5	2–10	6	P
90 × 120	150	54	5.6	11	4	2–8	6	P
4 × 5	150	54	4	8	8	2–15	7	A

Table 5.7 continued

Format (mm)	Focal length (mm)	Field of view (degree)	Maximum aperture (*f*-no)	Optimum aperture (*f*-no)	Standard magnification	Magnification range	Number of elements	Design type
130 × 180 (5 × 7 inch)	180	54	5.6	11	4	2–8	6	P
180 × 240 (8 × 10 inch)	240	54	5.6	11	3	1–6	6	P

DG, double Gauss. A, apochromat, RT, reverse Tessar. T, Tessar. WA, wide-angle. P, Plasmat.

Table 5.8 Lens fittings for 35 mm cameras

Name	Type	Register or flange focal distance (mm)	Variants	Compatible systems	Status
Alpha	B	37.8			D
Canon S	S 39 mm	28.8		Leica S	D
Canon	E, F	42.1	FD, FL, R		C
Cannon AF	B				C
Contax/Kiev	B	38.8		Nikon S	D
Contax/Yashica	B	45.5			C
Contarex	B	46.0			D
Exakta	B	44.7		Topcon D	D
Fujica	S 42 mm	45.5		Pentax S	O
Fujica X	B				C
Leica S	S 39 mm	28.8		Cannon S	O
Leica M	B	27.8	M2, M3, M4, CL	Minolta CLE	C
Leica R	B	46.9	3	Leicaflex	O, C
Mamiya SX	S 42 mm			Pentax S	O
Mamiya ZE	B		ES, NC		C, O
Minolta	B	43.5	MD, MC		C

Table 5.8 continued

Name	Type	Register or flange focal distance (mm)	Variants	Compatible systems	Status
Minolta AF	B				C
Miranda	V	41.5			D
Nikon	B	46.5	F, AI, E, AI-S, D	Ricoh Singlex	C
Nikon AF	B				C
Olympus AF	B				C
Olympus FTL	S 42 mm				O
Olympus OM	B	46.0			C
Pentax S	S 42 mm		ES	Chinon, Praktica, Petri, Ricoh, etc	O
Pentax K	B	45.5	Autofocus		C
Pentax KAF2	B				C
Ricoh XR	B	45.5		Pentax X	C
Rollei SL	B	44.5			D
Rollei QB	B			Voigtlander	C
Yashica AF	B				C
Zenith S	S 39 mm				D
Zenith B	S 42 mm				C

S, screw. B, bayonet. E, breech lock. F, breech/bayonet. V, variant. C, current. O, obsolescent. D, discontinued.

Table 5.9 Series filter sizes

Series number	Nominal diameter (mm)
4	20.8
4½	25.4
5	30
5½	36
6	41.3
7	50.8
8	62.5
8½	75
9	82.4
10	107

Table 5.10 Lens flare values

Flare level	Glare index (%)	Camera lens types
Low	0.0–1.4	Multi-coated standard, wide-angle and telephoto lenses. All lenses in low-flare situations
Moderate	1.5–4.4	Most single-layer coated lenses. Multi coated extreme wide-angle and telephoto lenses
High	4.5–6.4	Zoom lenses at large apertures. Old-style single-coated lenses, especially wide-angle types. Single-coated extreme wide-angle lenses
Very high	6.5–10	Old uncoated lenses. Zoom lenses at small apertures. Long-focus lenses in high-flare conditions.

Table 5.11 Theoretical resolution limits at various wavelengths

Effective *f*-number (N')	Resolution (cycles mm^{-1}) e line (λ = 546.1 nm)	g line (λ = 435.8 nm)	h line (λ = 404.7 nm)
1	1500	1880	2025
1.2	1250	1567	1688
1.4	1070	1343	1447
2	750	940	1013
2.8	535	672	723
4	375	470	505
5.6	270	336	362
8	190	235	253
11	135	170	184
16	95	118	127
22	68	85	92

Table 5.12 Properties of high-resolution lenses

Manu-facturer	Lens name	f (mm)	N	λ	Object to image distance (mm)	Image diameter (mm)	m	N'	NA	Diffraction limit of resolution (cycles mm^{-1})	Depth of focus ± (μm)	Depth of field ± (μm)	MTF (%) 250	MTF (%) 500	MTF (%) 1000	Distortion ± (μm)
Zeiss	S-Planar	14	1.6	436 ± 15	315 ± 3	4	1/20	1.63	0.31	1410	2.3	920	55	35	10	0.05
Zeiss	S-Planar	25	1.6	546 ± 10	315 ± 3	8	1/10	1.78	0.28	1030	3.4	340	45	25	–	
				436 ± 10						1290	2.8	280	50	30	–	
				405 ± 10						1390	2.6	260	55	35	–	0.1
Zeiss	S-Planar	100	2.8	546 (490–650)	1195	28	1/10	3.12	0.16	585	11	1100	–	–	–	1.0
Zeiss	S-Planar	70	2.2	395–445	315	17.6	1/4	2.78	0.18	890	6.3	100	50	20	–	0.4
Zeiss	S-Planar	125	2.8	436 ± 5 (546)	440	38	1/2	4.1	0.123	560	15	60	35	–	–	3
Zeiss	S-Planar	195	4	546 ± 30	4300 ± 30	90	1/20	4.2	0.12	435	19.5	7800	15	–	–	5
Zeiss	S-Planar	210	2	405 (546)	–	58	1	4	0.125	620	13	13	40	–	–	0.5
Tropel	Micro-Tropar	27	1.4	365 ± 5	315	4.2	1/10		0.4				82	62	–	1
Tropel	Micro-Tropar	27	1.6	405–436	315	7	1/10		0.285	1000			70	50	15	1

Table 5.12 continued

Manu-facturer	Lens name	f (mm)	N	λ	Object to image distance (mm)	Image diameter (mm)	m	N'	NA	Diffraction limit of resolution (cycles mm^{-1})	Depth of focus ± (μm)	Depth of field ± (μm)	MTF (%) 250	500	1000	Distortion ± (μm)
Nikon	Ultra Micro-Nikkor	30	1.2	546	810	2	1/25			1250						−1.3%
Nikon	Ultra Micro-Nikkor	28	1.8	546		8	1/10			650						
Nikon	Micro-Nikkor	150	5.6	400–650	1815	115	1/10			150						0.1%
Nikon	Repro-Nikkor	85	1	400–650	224	43	1	2		200						0

Table 5.13 Properties of perspective control lenses

Lens name	Focal length (mm)	Maximum aperture	Nominal format (mm)	Image circle diameter (mm)	Format diagonal (mm)	Field of view (degrees)	Normal field of View for format (degrees)	Maximum shift (vertical/ horizontal, mm)	Tilt (degrees)	Notes
Olympus Shift Lens	24	3.5	24 × 36	57	43	100	84	10/8	–	S
PC Nikkor	28	3.5	24 × 36	58	43	92	74	11/8	–	N
PC Nikkor	35	2.8	24 × 26	58	43	78	62	11/8	–	N
PA Curtagon-R	35	2.8	24 × 36	54	43	75	62	7/7	–	N
Canon TS	35	2.8	24 × 36	58	43	79	62	11/8	±8	T
Cannon TS-E	24	3.5	24 × 36	57	43	100	84	11/8	±8	
Cannon TS-E	45	2.8	24 × 36	57	43	67	51	11/8	±8	
Cannon TS-E	90	2.8	24 × 36	57	43	42	26	11/8	±8	
Mamiya Sekor Shift C	50	4	45 × 60	97	70	88	70	16/13	–	N
Super Angulon PCS	55	4.5	45 × 60	104	70	85	61	12/12	±10	A, F
Mamiya Sekor Z	75	4.5	60 × 70	124	90	79	62	30/20	–	A, F
SMC Pentax Shift	75	4.5	60 × 70	124	90	79	62	20/20	–	N

N, non-automatic. A, automatic. F, floating element. T, degree of tilt depends on amount of shift used. S, aspheric element used.

Table 5.14 Covering power and permissible lateral displacement of representative wide-angle lenses for view cameras

Lens name	Focal length (mm)	Maximum aperture (*f*-no.)	Nominal format	Format diagonal (mm)	Field of view on format diagonal (deg (*f*-no.))	Lens-covering power as FOV (deg (*f*-no.))	Image circle diameter (mm (*f*-no.))	Possible lateral shift at infinity focus vert./horiz. (mm (*f*-no.))
Nikkor-W	150	5.6	4 × 5 inch	154	54 (5.6)	60 (5.6)	174 (5.6)	10/8 (5.6)
						70 (22)	210 (22)	38/33 (22)
Super Angulon	65	5.6	4 × 5 inch	154	92 (5.6)	92 (5.6)	135 (5.6)	None (5.6)
					100 (22)	105 (22)	170 (22)	5/4 (22)
Nikkor-SW	65	4	4 × 5 inch	154	80 (4)	80 (4)	110 (4)	None (5.6)
					100 (16)	105 (16)	179 (16)	5/4 (16)
Super Angulon	75	5.6	4 × 5 inch	154	92 (5.6)	92 (5.6)	156 (5.6)	None (5.6)
						106 (22)	198 (22)	31/27 (22)
Nikkor-SW	75	4.5	4 × 5 inch	154	80 (4.5)	80 (4.5)	126 (4.5)	None (4.5)
					92 (16)	106 (16)	200 (16)	28/24 (16)
Super Angulon	90	5.6	4 × 5 inch	154	81 (5.6)	92 (5.6)	187 (5.6)	24/20 (5.6)
						105 (22)	235 (22)	53/47 (22)
Nikkor-SW	90	4.5	4 × 5 inch	154	80 (4.5)	80 (4.5)	154 (4.5)	None (4.5)
						105 (16)	235 (16)	48/42 (16)
Super Angulon	90	8	4 × 5 inch	154	81 (8)	92 (8)	187 (8)	24/20 (8)
						100 (22)	215 (22)	41/36 (22)
Super Angulon	165	8	8 × 10 inch	312	87 (8)	92 (8)	342 (8)	22/18 (8)
						100 (22)	393 (22)	57/49 (22)
Super Angulon	47	5.6	60 × 70 mm	91	88 (5.6)	92 (5.6)	98 (5.6)	5/4 (5.6)
						105 (22)	123 (22)	26/26 (22)

Table 5.15 Covering power of lenses for 4 × 5 format

Date of introduction	Type of lens	Name of lens	FOV (degrees)	f(mm)	N	Image circle diameter (mm)	Shifts for infinity focus and $f/22$ (mm)
1930	WA	Angulon	80	90	6.8	152	9/7
1955	WA	Super Angulon	100	90	8	214	50/43
1964	WA	Super Angulon	105	90	5.6	236	62/53
1990	WA	Super Angulon XL	110	90	5.6	259	75/66
1990	EWA	Super Angulon XL	100	58	5.6	152	9/7
1992	WA	Grandagon-N	105	90	4.5	236	54/48
	EWA	Grandagon-N	105	65	4.5	170	12/10
	S	Sironar-N	72	150	5.6	214	41/36
1992	S	Apo Sironar-N	72	150	5.6	214	41/36
1992	S	Apo Sironar-S	72	150	5.6	231	50/45
1992	S	Apo Sironar-W	75	150	5.6	252	63/56
1992	S	Super-Symmar HM	80	150	5.6	254	64/58
	S	Symmar-S	80	150	5.6	210	38/33
	LF	Apo Ronar	70	240	9	212	45/39
1990	S	Macro-Sironar-N	48	210	5.6	525*	208/198*
1990	S	Apo-Symmar	64	150	5.6	220	44/39

*When focused for life-size reproduction (unit magnification)
WA, wide-angle, EWA, extreme WA. S, standard, LF, long focus.

Table 5.16 Projection formulae for lenses

Name	Projection formula	y_{max} (mm)	Image circle diameter (mm)	Format (mm)	θ_{max} (degrees)	f (mm)	Typical value of f (mm)
Rectilinear	$y = f \tan \theta$	21.5	43	24 × 36	60	12.4	13
		40	80	56 × 56	45	40	38
Equidistant	$y = f\theta$	21.5	43	24 × 36	90	13.7	16
		11.5	23	24 × 36	90	7.32	8
		11.5	23	24 × 36	110	5.99	6
		40	80	56 × 56	90	25	30
Equi-solid angle (orthographic)	$y = 2f \sin (\theta/2)$	11.5	23	24 × 36	90	8.1	8
Stereographic	$y = 2f \tan(\theta/2)$	11.5	23	24 × 36	90	5.8	–

Table 5.17 Image height (y) for fisheye lenses

θ	y as a multiple of f					
(degrees)	Rectilinear	Δy	Equidistant	Δy	Equi-solid angle	Δy
10	0.176	0.176	0.175	0.175	0.174	0.174
20	0.364	0.188	0.348	0.174	0.347	0.173
30	0.577	0.213	0.524	0.175	0.518	0.171
40	0.839	0.262	0.698	0.174	0.684	0.162
50	1.192	0.353	0.873	0.175	0.845	0.161
60	1.732	0.540	1.047	0.174	1.000	0.155
70	2.748	1.575	1.222	0.175	1.147	0.147
80	5.671	2.923	1.396	0.174	1.286	0.139
90	∞	∞	1.571	0.175	1.141	0.128
100	–	–	1.745	0.174	–	–
110	–	–	1.920	0.175	–	–

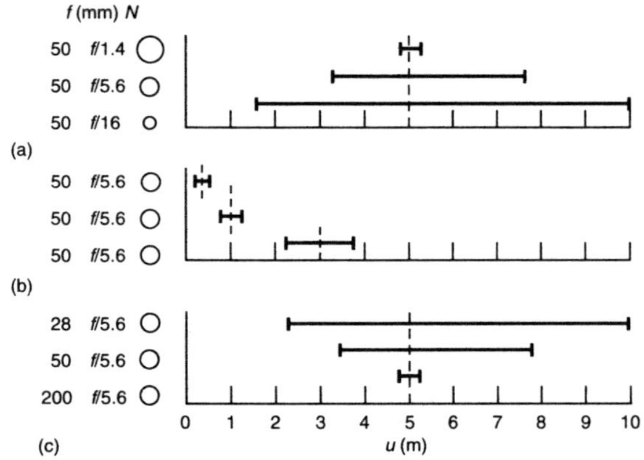

Fig. 5.18 Depth of Field
Effect of the variables focal length (f), f-number (N) and focused distance (u) at constant value for circle of confusion (C).
(a) Lens aperture varying from $f/1.4$ to $f/16$ with 50 mm lens focused on 5 m. (b) Focused distance varying from 0.5 to 3 m with 50 mm lens at $f/5.6$. (c) Focal length varying from 28 to 200 mm at $f/5.6$ focused on 5 m.

Table 5.19 Circle of confusion values

Format	Circle of confusion diameter (mm)
8 × 10 inch	0.20
5 × 7 inch	0.14
4 × 5 inch	0.10
60 × 90 mm	0.075
60 × 60 mm	0.03–0.06
24 × 36 mm	0.02–0.033
35 mm cine	0.025–0.05
16 mm cine	0.025–0.013
8 mm cine	0.02
1.25 inch video	0.04
1 inch video	0.03
⅔ inch viceo	0.021–0.02
½ inch video	0.016–0.015

Table 5.20 Summary of formulae for image sharpness

Term	Symbols	Formula (accurate)	Formula (approximate)
Object conjugate distance distance of plane of sharp focus	*u, L*	$u = f(1 + 1/m)$	
Image conjugate distance bellows extension	*v, L'*	$v = f(1 + /m); f + e$	
Focusing extension	*e*	$v - f$; mu $- f$; mf	
Near point of depth of field	*R*	$\frac{uf^2}{f^2 + NCu}$	$\frac{Hu}{H + u}$
Far point of depth of field	*S*	$\frac{uf^2}{f^2 - \mathrm{NCu}}$	$\frac{Hu}{H - u}$
Depth of field (distant subjects)	*T*	$\frac{2f^2u^2NC}{f^4 - N^2C^2u^2}$	$\frac{2u^2NC}{f^2}$
Hyperfocal distance Over focal distance (video)	*H*	$\frac{f^2}{NC}$	
Near zone of sharpness (per cent) (u – R)	*Y*	$f - NC - \frac{NC}{m} - \frac{N^2C^2}{f} - \frac{N^2C^2}{f^2m^2}$	$\frac{f - \frac{NC}{m}}{2f}$

Table 5.20 continued

Term	Symbols	Formula (accurate)	Formula (approximate)
Far zone of sharpness (per cent) (S – u)	X	$f + NC - \frac{NC}{m} - \frac{N^2C^2}{f} - \frac{N^2C^2}{f^2m^2}$	$\frac{f + \frac{NC}{m}}{2f}$
Close-up depth of field	T	$\frac{2CN(1+m)}{m^2}$	
Depth of focus	t	$\frac{2CN\nu}{f}$	Tm^2; $2CN$ (for m small)

C, circle of confusion. m, magnification. N, f-number. f, focal length

Table 5.21 Construction of a zone focusing scale

Focus scale setting (m)	*u*	*S*	*R*	*T*(m)
∞	∞	∞	*h*	–
20	*h*	∞	*h*/2	maximum
10	*h*/2	*h*	*h*/3	13.3
6.67	*h*/3	*h*/2	*h*/4	5
5	*h*/4	*h*/3	*h*/5	2.67
4	*h*/5	*h*/4	*h*/6	1.67
3.33	*h*/6	*h*/5	*h*/7	1.14
2.86	*h*/7	*h*/6	*h*/8	0.83

Data: $f = 100$ mm, $N = f/10$, C = 0.05 mm, $h = 20$ m. Focus settings of ∞, 20 m, 6.67 m, 4 m, 2.86 m, cover the full zone from infinity to 2.5 m.
h, hyperfocal distance. T, depth of field. u, focused distance. S, far point of sharpness. R, rear point of sharpness.

Table 5.22 Depth of field tables. Data for 50 mm and 150 mm lenses for the 60 × 60 mm format. (Bronica data)
50 mm *f*/3.5

	Distance (feet)										
Aperture	∞	30	15	10	7	5	4	3	2.5	2	1.75
3.5	∞	124	23.8	13.2	8.36	5.62	4.37	3.19	2.5	2	1.75
	39.1	17.2	11.0	8.08	6.03	4.51	3.69	2.84	2.39	1.94	1.70
4	∞	192	25.5	13.6	8.55	5.70	4.42	3.21	2.64	2.08	1.80
	35.2	16.3	10.7	7.92	5.94	4.46	3.66	2.82	2.38	1.93	1.70
5.6	∞	∞	36.0	16.1	9.42	6.06	4.62	3.31	2.70	2.11	1.83
	25.0	13.8	9.55	7.30	5.60	4.27	3.54	2.75	2.33	1.90	1.68
8	∞	∞	87.7	21.7	11.0	6.65	4.94	3.46	2.79	2.16	1.86
	17.8	11.3	8.32	6.57	5.18	4.03	3.38	2.66	2.27	1.86	1.65
11	∞	∞	∞	42.9	14.5	7.73	5.48	3.69	2.93	2.24	1.91
	12.6	9.05	7.05	5.77	4.68	3.74	3.18	2.54	2.19	1.81	1.62
16	∞	∞	∞	∞	27.0	10.1	6.51	4.10	3.16	2.36	1.99
	9.02	7.07	5.81	4.93	4.13	3.39	2.93	2.39	2.09	1.75	1.57
22	∞	∞	∞	∞	∞	18.0	8.94	4.87	3.57	2.55	2.12
	6.47	5.43	4.68	4.11	3.55	3.01	2.65	2.22	1.96	1.67	1.51

Table 5.22 continued 150 mm *f*/3.5

	Distance (feet)										
Aperture	∞	50	30	20	15	12	10	8	7	6	5
3.5	∞	58.3	32.7	21.2	15.6	12.4	10.3	8.16	7.12	6.08	5.05
	341	43.8	27.7	19.0	14.4	11.6	9.76	7.84	6.88	5.92	4.95
4	∞	59.4	33.1	21.3	15.7	12.4	10.3	8.18	7.13	6.09	5.06
	308	43.2	27.5	18.9	14.4	11.6	9.73	7.83	6.88	5.91	4.94
5.6	∞	64.4	34.6	21.9	16.0	12.6	10.4	8.25	7.18	6.13	5.08
	218	40.9	26.5	18.4	14.1	11.5	9.62	7.77	6.83	5.88	4.92
8	∞	73.2	36.9	22.8	16.5	12.9	10.6	8.36	7.26	6.18	5.12
	154	38.0	25.3	17.9	13.8	11.2	9.47	6.67	6.76	5.83	4.89
11	∞	90.7	40.8	24.1	17.2	13.3	10.9	8.52	7.38	6.26	5.17
	109	34.6	23.8	17.1	13.3	10.9	9.27	7.55	6.66	5.76	4.84
16	∞	137	47.9	26.4	18.2	13.9	11.3	8.75	7.55	6.38	5.25
	77.4	30.7	21.9	16.1	12.8	10.6	9.00	7.37	6.53	5.67	4.78
22	∞	505	63.8	30.5	20.1	14.9	11.9	9.11	7.81	6.56	5.35
	54.8	26.5	19.7	14.9	12.0	10.1	8.65	7.14	6.35	5.54	5.70

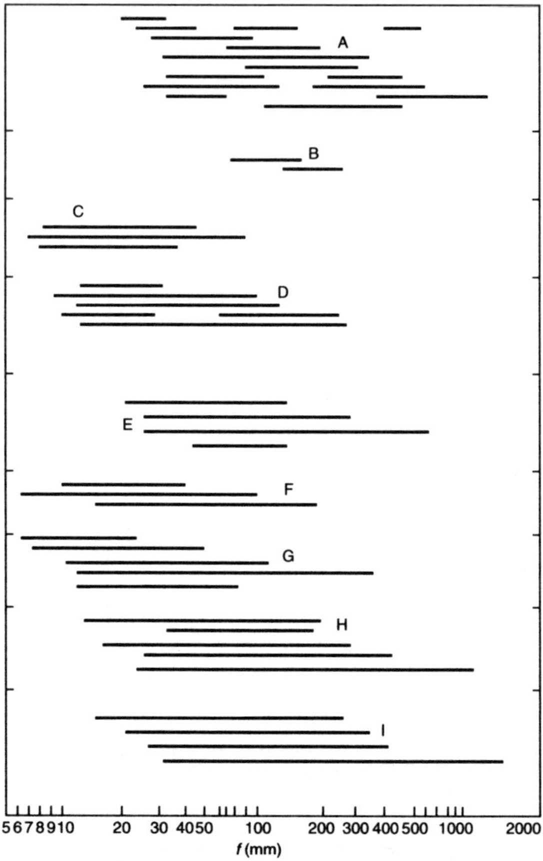

Figure 5.23 Zoom Ratios for Various Formats
A, 24 × 36 mm format. B, 60 × 60 mm. C, Super 8 mm cine. D, 16 mm/Super 16 mm cine. E, 35 mm cine. F, ½ inch video. G, ⅔ inch video. H, 1 inch video. I, 1¼ inch video.

Table 5.24 Use of attachments to vary focal length range

Aperture used	Focal length range (mm)	Zoom ratio	Maximum aperture
None – unaided lens	9–135	15 : 1	f/1.5–1.9
× 2 range extender (RE)	18–270	15 : 1	f/3–3.8
× 1.66 tele-zoom (TZ)	64–225	3.5 : 1	f/1.9
RE + TZ	30–450	15 : 1	f/3–3.8
× 0.8 retro-zoom (RZ)	7.2–108	15 : 1	f/1.5–1.9
RE + RZ	14.5–216	14.9 : 1	f/3–3.8

Table 5.25 Varifocal projection lenses

Format	Focal length range (mm)	Aperture	Configurations (elements/ groups)
23 × 35	70–125	2.8	11/10
23 × 35	127–254	3.5	10/9
16 mm	30–70	1.3	13/11
16 mm	20–60	1.8	13/9
Super 8 mm	11–30	1.1	6/5

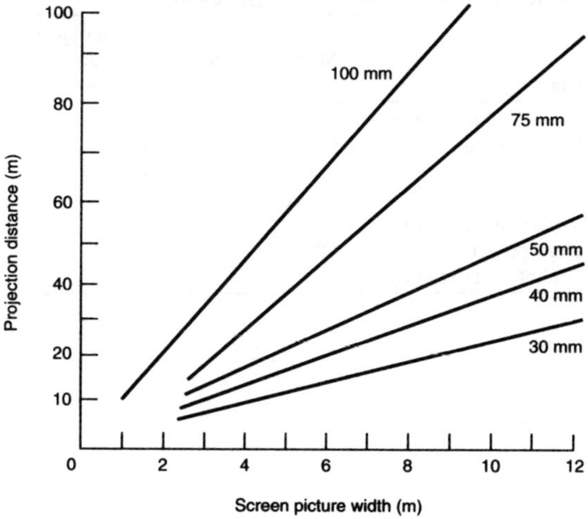

Figure 5.26 Projected Picture Sizes for 35 mm Cine

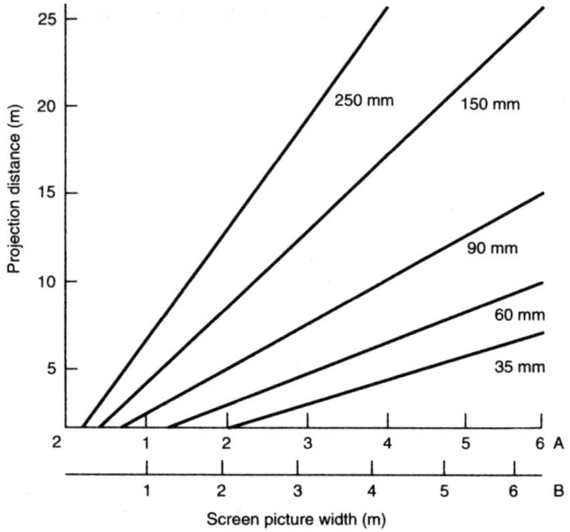

Figure 5.27 Projected Picture Sizes for Slide Projectors
Scale A is for horizontal 24 × 36 mm format. Scale B is for 40 × 40 mm format.

Table 5.28 Photography and magnification

Class	Magnification range	Typical object conjugate range (mm)
General photography	< 0.1	∞ –1000
Close-up photography	0.1–1.0	1000–10
Photomacrography	1.0–50	10–2
Low-power photomicrography	20–100	5–1
High-power photomicrography	50–1500	8– < 0.1

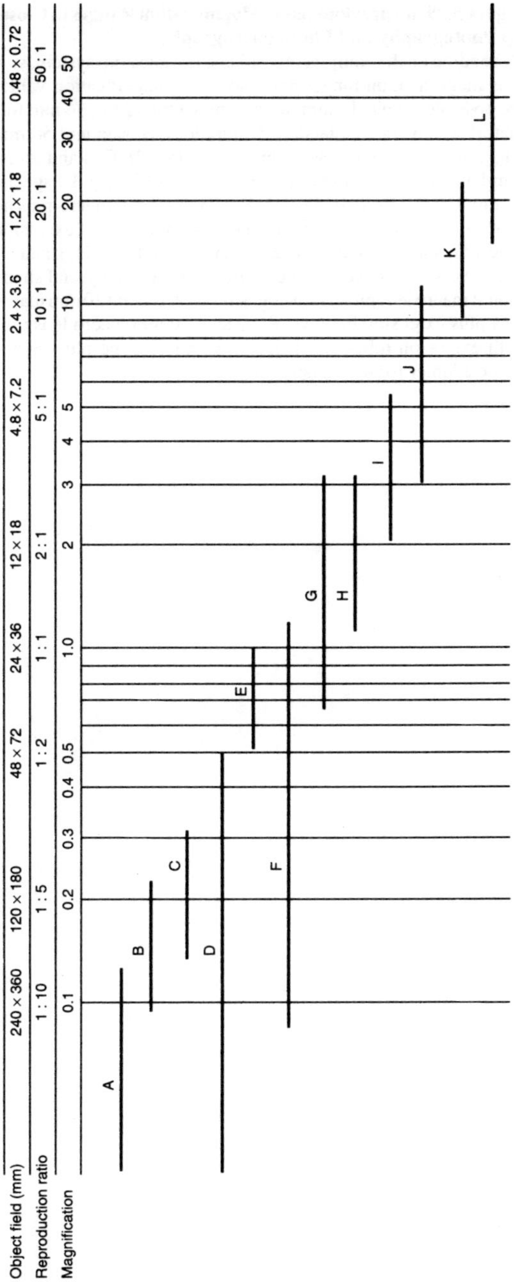

Object field (mm)
240 × 360
120 × 180
48 × 72
24 × 36
12 × 18
4.8 × 7.2
2.4 × 3.6
1.2 × 1.8
0.48 × 0.72
Reproduction ratio
1 : 10
1 : 5
1 : 2
1 : 1
2 : 1
5 : 1
10 : 1
20 : 1
50 : 1
Magnification
0.1
0.2
0.3
0.4
0.5
1.0
2
3
4
5
10
20
30
40
50
A
B
C
D
E
F
G
H
I
J
K
L

Figure 5.29 (on previous page) Magnification Ranges in Close-up Photography and Photomacrography

Depending on the equipment available in a close-up system, various magnification ranges and maximum magnification values are possible. Typical examples are shown for a 24 × 36 mm format SLR camera. A, standard 50 mm lens. B, standard 50 mm lens plus a +2 dioptre close-up lens (0.10–0.2). C, standard 50 mm lens plus a +3 dioptre close-up lens (0.15–0.3). D, special 50 mm macro lens (to 0.5). E, special 50 mm macro lens plus an extension tube (0.5–1.0). F, standard lens plus a set of extension tubes. G, standard lens plus an extension bellows. H, standard lens reverse-mounted on an extension bellows. I, special short-mount macro lens plus extension bellows. J, special 20 mm macro lens plus extension bellows. K, special 20 mm macro lens plus both extension tubes and bellows. L, microscope plus microscope adapter for the camera body.

Table 5.30 Lenses for Photomacrography

Manufacturer	Focal length (mm)	Maximum aperture	Aperture numbers	Magnification range (best performance)	Mounting thread
A	16	f/2.5	1,2,4,8,15,30	10× – 40×	RMS
	25	f/3.5	1,2,4,8,15,30	6.3× – 25×	RMS
	40	f/4.5	1,2,4,8,15,30	4 × – 16×	RMS
	63	f/4.5	1,2,4,8,15,30	2 × – 10×	RMS
	100	f/6.3	1,2,4,8,15,30	0.8 × – 8 ×	M35 × 0.75
B	12.5	f/1.9	1.9, 2.8, 3.5, 4, 5.6, 8	15× – 30×	RMS
	25	f/2.5	2.5, 3.5, 4, 5.6, 8, 11, 16	7× – 16×	RMS
	50	f/4.0	4, 5.6, 8, 11, 16, 22, 32	3× – 8×	RMS
	50	f/2.8	2.8, 3.5, 4, 5.6, 8, 11, 16, 22	3× – 8×	M40 × 0.75
	80	f/4.5	4.5, 5.6, 8, 11, 16, 22, 32	1× – 4×	M40 × 0.75
	120	f/5.6	5.6, 8, 11, 16, 22, 32	0.5× – 2×	M40 × 0.75
C	19	f/2.8	1, 2, 3, 4, 5, 6	15× – 40×	RMS
	35	f/4.5	1, 2, 3, 4, 5, 6	8× – 20×	RMS
	65	f/4.5	1, 2, 3, 4, 5, 6	3.5× – 10×	M39 × 1.0
	120	f/6.3	1, 2, 3, 4, 5, 6, 7	0.3× – 4×	M39 × 1.0

Table 5.31 Properties of macro lenses (Zeiss data)

Zeiss Luminar lens	Optimum magnification (for $v = 250$ mm)	Usable magnification range	Maximum diameter of subject (mm)
16 mm *f*/2.5	14	10–40	5–6
25 mm *f*/3.5	8.8	6–25	10–12
40 mm *f*/4.5	5	4–16	20–25
63 mm *f*/4.5	3	2–10	30–40
100 mm *f*/6.3	2	0.8–8	70–75

Table 5.32 Close-up photography and photomacrography

Additional lens extension (e) $e = f^2/(u - f)$	Total extension (bellows extension) $v = f(1 + m)$	Image magnification $m = v/f - 1$	Reproduction ratio	Lens to subject distance $u = v/m$	Film to subject distance $R = u + v$ $= f(2 + m + 1/m)$	Subject area covered $A \propto 1/m^2$	Effective aperture $N = N(1 + m)$	Relative image illumination $E \propto 1/(N')^2$
0	f	0 (infinity focus)	0 : 1	∞	∞	–	N	1.0
0.25f	1.25f	0.25	1 : 4	5f	6.25f	16A	1.25N	0.64
0.5f	1.5f	0.5	1 : 2	3f	4.5f	4A	1.5	0.44
f	2f	1.0	1 : 1	2f	4f	A	2N	0.25
1.5f	2.5f	1.5	1.5 : 1	1.67f	4.17f	0.44A	2.5N	0.16
2f	3f	2.0	2 : 1	1.5f	4.5f	0.25A	3N	0.11
3f	4f	3.0	3 : 1	1.33f	5.33f	0.11A	4N	0.063
5f	6f	5.0	5 : 1	1.2f	7.2f	0.04A	6N	0.028
10f	11f	10.0	10 : 1	1.1f	12.1f	0.01A	11N	0.008
20f	21f	20.0	20 : 1	1.05f	20.05f	0.003A	21N	0.002
30f	31f	30.0	30 : 1	1.03f	32.03f	0.001A	31N	0.001
40f	41f	40.0	40 : 1	1.025f	42.03f	0.0006A	41N	0.0006
50f	51f	50.0	50 : 1	1.02f	52.02f	0.0004A	51N	0.0004

Table 5.33 Exposure Compensation
Compensation factor = $(M + 1)^2$

Image to subject ratio	Compensation factor	Image to subject ratio	Compensation factor
1:20	1.10	1:1	4
1:19	1.11	1.25:1	5
1:18	1.11	1.50:1	6
1:17	1.12	1.75:1	7.5
1:16	1.13	2:1	9
1:15	1.14	2.25:1	10.5
1:14	1.15	2.5:1	12
1:13	1.16	2.75:1	14
1:12	1.17	3:1	16
1:11	1.19	3.5:1	20
1:10	1.21	4:1	25
1:9	1.24	4.5:1	30
1:8	1.27	5:1	36
1:7	1.31	6:1	49
1:6	1.36	7:1	64
1:5	1.44	8:1	81
1:4.5	1.50	9:1	100
1:4	1.56	10:1	121
1:3	1.78	12:1	169
1:2.75	1.86	13:1	196
1:2.5	1.96	14:1	225
1:2.25	2.09	15:1	256
1:2	2.25	16:1	289
1:75	2.47	17:1	324
1:5	2.78	18:1	361
1:25	3.24	19:1	400
1:1	4.00	20:1	441

Table 5.34 Long focus lenses for close-up photography

Focal length (mm)	Design	Minimum focusing distance (m)	(ft)	Magnifi-cation	Repro-duction ratio
200	Micro	0.58	1.92	1	1 : 1
120–300	Zoom	0.65	2.08	0.77	1 : 1.3
70–250	Zoom	0.95	3.08	0.4	1 : 2.5
400	Apochromat	3	9.8	0.14	1 : 7.2
400	Catadioptric	2	6.6	0.23	1 : 4.3
600	Catadioptric	2	6.6	0.33	1 : 3
1000	Catadioptric	5	16.4	0.22	1 : 4.6

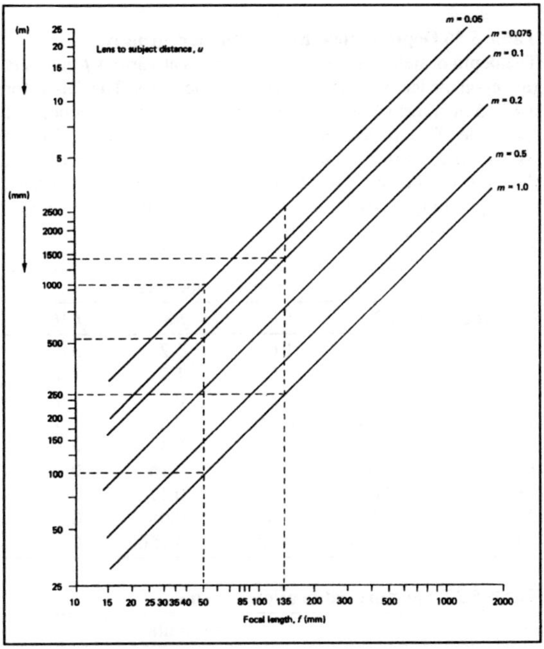

Figure 5.35 Working Distances for Close-up Focusing
The graph shows the lens to subject distance (u) for magnifications in the close-up range of 0.05–1.0. Most lenses focus to give a maximum magnification of 0.1, when exposure corrections begin to become significant. The example for a 50 mm and a 135 mm lens give this value at distances of approximately 500 mm and 1.5 m respectively.

Table 5.36 Depth of field for photomacrography.
The depth of field is shown in millimetres at various *f*-numbers (as set on the lens) and at various magnifications. The data is for a 4 × 5 inch format using a value of 0.1 mm for the diameter of the circle of confusion. For the 60 × 70 mm and 24 × 36 mm formats using values of 0.06 mm and 0.033 mm respectively, the value can be multiplied by 0.6 and 0.33 respectively to give corresponding values. Other values can be interpolated from this table. Formula used:
$T = 2CN(1 + m)m^2$.

	Relative aperture			
Magnification	*f*/2	*f*/4	*f*/8	*f*/16
1	0.8	1.6	3.2	6.4
2	0.3	0.6	1.2	2.4
3	0.18	0.35	0.7	1.4
4	0.13	0.25	0.5	1.0
5	0.1	0.2	0.4	0.8
10	0.04	0.08	0.16	0.32
15	0.03	0.06	0.11	0.22
20	0.02	0.03	0.08	0.16
30	0.014	0.028	0.056	0.11

Table 5.37 Aperture calibration systems

Origin	Formula
Relative aperture	$N = f/e$
Zeiss (Rudolph)	$K = 10\,000N^{-2}$
Zeiss (Rudolph)	$K = 2500N^{-2}$
Paris 1899	$K = N^2/100$
Dallmeyer and Stolz	$K = N^2/10$
Paris 1900	$K = N^2$
Uniform Series (RPS 1881)	$K = N^2/16$
Aperture value (APEX system)	$K = \log_2 N^2$
T-number	$K = N/T^{1/2}$
Photometric aperture or G-number	$K = 4N^2T$
f-number	$f\text{-number} = 2^{N/2}$

f, focal length. *e*, entrance pupil diameter. *N*, relative aperture. *T*, transmittance. *K*, engraved value.

Table 5.38 Equivalent aperture value calibrations

Pupil relative area	International scale	Continental scale	Alternative scale	APEX aperture value	US system of RPS	Stolz stop numbers	Dallmeyer, Goerz and Voigtlander	Exposure factor
8192	1			0				1
		1.1						
			1.2					
4096	1.4			1				2
		1.6						
			1.8					
2048	2			2				4
		2.2						
			2.5					
1024	2.8			3				8
		3.3				1	1	
			3.5					
512	4			4	1			16
		4.5				2	2	
			5					
256	5.6			5	2	3		32

Table 5.38 continued

Pupil relative area	International scale	Continental scale	Alternative scale	APEX aperture value	US system of RPS	Stolz stop numbers	Dallmeyer, Goerz and Voigtlander	Exposure factor
		6.3				4		
			7			5		
128	8			6	4	6		64
		9					8	
			10					
64	11			7	8	12		128
		12.5					16	
			14					
32	16			8	16	24		256
		18					32	20
			20					
16	22			9	32			512
		25				64		
			28					
8	32			10	64			1024
		36					128	
			40					

Table 5.38 continued

Pupil relative area	International scale	Continental scale	Alternative scale	APEX aperture value	US system of RPS	Stolz stop numbers	Dallmeyer, Goerz and Voigtlander	Exposure factor
4	45			11	128			2048
		50						
			56					
2	64			12				4096
		72						
			80					
1	90							8192
0.5	128							16 384

Table 5.39 Lens pupil factors (Zeiss data)

Focal Length (mm)	Aperture	Format (mm)	Construction	Entrance Pupil diameter *En* (mm)	Exit pupil diameter *Ex* (mm)	Pupil factor (magnification) $P = Ex/En$	Exposure increase factor at $m = 1.0$
30	3.5	60 × 60	Quasi-fisheye	8.5	29.9	3.52	1.65
40	4	60 × 60	Retrofocus	10.2	24.1	2.36	2.03
38	4.5	60 × 60	Symmetrical	8.6	9.1	1.06	3.78
50	2.8	60 × 60	Retrofocus	18.2	32.1	1.76	2.46
80	2.8	60 × 60	Double Gauss	28.8	34.5	1.20	3.36
110	2	60 × 60	Double Gauss	53.8	58.4	1.09	3.68
120	4	60 × 60	Double Gauss (macro)	29.7	33.5	1.13	3.55
150	2.8	60 × 60	Telephoto	52.5	38.2	0.73	5.62
250	4	60 × 60	Telephoto	61.5	29.4	0.48	9.51
500	4.5	60 × 60	Mirror	128	66.2	0.52	8.54
1000	5.6	60 × 60	Mirror	212	112	0.53	8.33
15	3.5	24 × 36	Retrofocus	4.3	15.5	3.61	1.63
25	2.8	24 × 36	Retrofocus	9.1	19.8	2.18	2.13
28	2	24 × 36	Retrofocus	14	31.8	2.27	1.86
35PC	2.8	24 × 36	Retrofocus	12.6	24.2	1.92	2.31

Table 5.39 continued

Focal Length (mm)	Aperture	Format (mm)	Construction	Entrance Pupil diameter *En* (mm)	Exit pupil diameter *Ex* (mm)	Pupil factor (magnification) $P = Ex/En$	Exposure increase factor at $m = 1.0$
45	2.8	24 × 36	Tessar	16.3	15.4	0.95	4.21
50	1.4	24 × 36	Double Gauss	36.2	49.7	1.37	2.99
60	2.8	24 × 36	Double Gauss (macro)	21.2	21.9	1.03	3.88
100	2	24 × 36	Double Gauss	50	46.9	0.94	4.26
135	2.8	24 × 36	Telephoto	47.8	31.5	0.66	6.33
200	4	24 × 36	Telephoto	50	21.4	0.43	11.06
300	4	24 × 36	Telephoto	75	32.8	0.44	10.71
40–80	4	24 × 36	Zoom	(40)11.6	(40)27.7	2.39	2.01
				(80)21.6	(80)25.3	1.17	3.44
70–210	3.5	24 × 36	Zoom	(70)19.9	(70)27	1.36	3.01
				(210)56	(210)27	0.48	9.51

Table 5.40 Properties of viewfinder systems

	Wire frame finder	Bright line frame finder	TLR	SLR and waist-level finder	SLR and pentaprism	View camera
Image Properties						
Image inverted	N	N	N	N	N	Y
Image reversed	N	N	Y	Y	N	Y
Image used for focusing	N	N	Y	Y	Y	Y
Image used for exposure measurement	N	N	Y	Y	Y	P
Image combined with a rangefinder or focusing aid	N	P	P	P	P	P
More than one subject outlined	P	P	N	N	N	N
Usable in very dim lighting	Y	Y	P	P	P	P
Eyesight problems	N	Y	Y	Y	Y	N
Time lag or response problems	N	N	N	Y	Y	Y
Eye-level use	Y	Y	P	N	Y	Y
Waist-level use	N	N	Y	Y	N	N
Parallax errors	Y	Y	Y	N	N	N

Table 5.40 continued

	Wire frame finder	Bright line frame finder	TLR	SLR and waist-level finder	SLR and pentaprism	View camera
Applications						
Sport and action	1	1	2, 3	2, 3	1	3
Children	1	1	1	2	2	3
Landscape	2	2	2	1	1	1
Architecture	2	2	3	2	2	1
Animals	1	1	1	1	1	3
Copying	3	3	2, 3	1	1	1
Still life	3	3	2, 3	1	1	1
Portraiture	2	2	1	1	1	2

Y, yes. N, no. P, possible. 1, Ideal. 2, possible. 3, not really suitable.

Table 5.41 Effective base lengths of camera rangefinders.

Camera	Viewfinder magnification (M_E)	Rangefinder base (*b*, mm)	Effective base length (*B*, mm)
Leica IIIc	1.5	39	58.5
Contax II	0.65	90	58.5
Leica M2/M4/M6	0.72	68.5	49.3
Leica M3	0.9	68.5	61.5
Leica M3 plus f35 mm lens	1.4	68.5	93.0
Leica M2/M6 ditto	1.0	68.5	68.5
Minolta CLE	0.58	49.6	28.8
Fujica GS645	0.63	39.5	24.9
Makina 67	0.67	63.0	42.2

Table 5.42 Practical Shutter Speeds for Moving Objects

Distance		Exposure Time (seconds) for Object Speed of								
ft	m	2 3.2	4 6.4	8 13	16 25	30 50	60 100	120 200	250 400	500 mph 800 kmph
1	0.3	1/3000	–	–	–	–	–	–	–	–
2	0.6	1/1500	1/3000	–	–	–	–	–	–	–
4	1.2	1/750	1/1500	1/3000	–	–	–	–	–	
8	2.4	1/400	1/750	1/1500	1/3000	–	–	–	–	–
16	4.8	1/200	1/400	1/750	1/1500	1/3000	–	–	–	–
32	10	1/100	1/200	1/400	1/750	1/1500	1/3000	–	–	–
64	20	1/50	1/100	1/200	1/400	1/750	1/1500	1/3000	–	–
125	40	1/25	1/50	1/100	1/200	1/400	1/750	1/1500	1/3000	–
250	80	1/10	1/25	1/50	1/100	1/200	1/400	1/750	1/1500	1/3000
500	150	1/5	1/10	1/25	1/50	1/100	1/200	1/400	1/750	1/1500
miles	km									
0.25	0.4	1/2	1/5	1/10	1/25	1/50	1/100	1/200	1/400	1/750
0.5	0.8	1	1/2	1/5	1/10	1/25	1/50	1/100	1/200	1/400
1.0	1.6	2	1	1/2	1/5	1/10	1/25	1/50	1/100	1/200

These shutter speeds apply for objects moving across the line of sight of the camera. For movement diagonally towards or away from the camera, the exposures may be 1–1/2 times as long (e.g., 1/500 second instead of 1/750). For movement directly towards or away from the camera 3 times as long exposures may be given (e.g., 1/250 second instead of 1/750). The standard of definition is 1/1000 of the focal length of the normal camera lens. With long focus or telephoto lenses the speeds must be multiplied (or the exposure time must be divided) by the power of the telephoto lens, e.g., 1/100 second becomes 1/200 with a 2× telephoto lens.

5.43 Supplementary close up lenses

Close-up lenses don't give as good-quality images as a macro lens, but they are inexpensive, compact and require no extra exposure. The power of a close-up lens is generally expressed in dioptres: dioptre power is equal to one over the focal length in metres. Calculating the new point of sharpest focus when a supplementary is fitted is not difficult—simply use the formula below to work out the focal length of the combination of lenses, then use the formulae given in Table 5.20 to determine the subject distance for any particular lens extension you are using.

When you fit all but the weakest close-up lenses, you'll find that the focusing action of the lens moves the point in sharp focus just a small distance. In practice, it is enough to know that, when the main lens is focused on infinity, the distance to the point in sharpest focus is equal to the focal length of the supplementary lens. So, for example, a + 2 dioptre close-up lens has a focal length of 1/2 metre, so the point in sharpest focus will be 50cm (about 20in) away when the lens is focused on infinity. Note that this rule holds true regardless of the focal length of the prime lens in use.

Combined focal length = (S × F)/(S + F)
where S is the focal length of the supplementary lens,
and F that of the main lens

Calculating magnification The simplest way to determine the necessary extra exposure for a macro is to use magnification. This is easy using the table opposite: simply place a ruler or tape at the subject position, with one end visible in the viewfinder at the extreme edge of the frame. Check where the other side of the frame cuts the rule, then read off the magnification from the chart. With 5 × 4 in film, place the rule parallel to the long dimension of the frame; with roll film, the rule crosses the film width. If you are using a symmetrical lens, you can also read off exposure compensation from the chart.

Bear in mind, though, that most viewing aids magnify and crop the image slightly, so if you judge magnification using this method, you may need to check whether your camera shows 100 percent of the image that will appear on film. You can do this by placing at the film plane a small piece of ground glass (or a plastic ruler) and comparing how much of the image is included at the film plane with the amount visible in the viewfinder. If you are using 35mm film, simply place the scale opposite close to the subject, so that it crosses the shorter dimension of the frame, and read off the magnification or exposure increase directly in the camera viewfinder.

Table 5.44 Magnification and Exposure compensation for larger formats

Magnification	Exposure factor	Exposure increase (stops)	Ruler scale 6 × 6cm	Ruler scale 5 × 4in
5:1	36	5	11mm	2.5cm
4.5:1	30	5	13mm	2.8cm
4:1	25	4½	15mm	3.2cm
3.5:1	20	4⅓	17mm	3.6cm
3:1	16	4	19mm	4.2cm
2.5:1	12	3½	23mm	5.0cm
2:1	9	3	29mm	6.3cm
1.5:1	6.25	2	39mm	8.4cm
1:1	4	2	58mm	13cm
1:1.25	3.24	1⅔	73mm	16cm
1:1.5	2.77	1½	87mm	19cm
1:1.75	2.46	1⅓	101mm	22cm
1:2	2.25	1	116mm	25cm
1:3	1.77	1	174mm	38cm
1:4	1.56	⅔	232mm	50cm
1:5	1.44	½	290mm	63cm
1:6	1.36	½	348mm	76cm
1:8	1:26	⅓	464mm	102cm
1:10	1.21	⅓	580mm	127cm
1:12	negligible		700mm	152cm

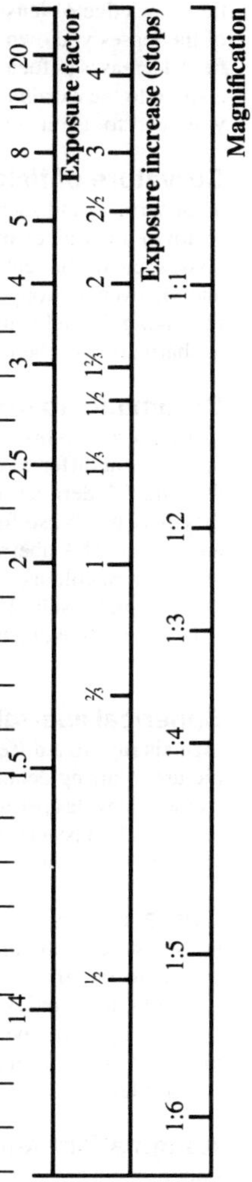

5.45 Lens aberrations

While there is nothing you can do about lens design itself, a little knowledge of lens aberrations can help you make the most of the lenses you own. For example, knowing that curvature of field decreases as focal length increases, you might choose to set a zoom to the extreme telephoto end of its focal length range if you need to use it for, say flat copying or other critical work.

Curvature of field A simple lens forms a curved image of a flat surface, and such an image will never be sharp across the width of a flat piece of film. In practical terms, this means that if you focus on the centre of the image, the corners will be unsharp, and vice versa. Stopping the lens down doesn't have the effect of making the field any flatter. What it does in fact is make the unsharp areas of the image somewhat less blurred.

Chromatic aberration Lenses suffering from axial chromatic aberration bring the different colour components of light to a focus at different distances from the lens, producing colour fringing. Modern lenses are usually well corrected for this, but they may be less so for what is known as transverse chromatic aberration. This aberration produces images of different sizes for different colours of off-axis rays and, again, colour fringing is the visual result. The problem is most acute with telephoto lenses–fluorite elements or catadioptric design provide a solution.

Spherical aberration Lenses with spherical surfaces bring off-axis rays to a different focus from those at the centre of the picture, blurring detail across the whole image. The aberration worsens at wide apertures, close subject distances and short focal lengths. The answer to the problem here is to avoid photographing close subjects with fast wide-angle lenses set at full aperture.

Coma This aberration is most obvious when points of light, such as streetlamps, appear in the image–when reproduced, they appear to be smeared into comma shapes instead of circles. Stopping down eases the problem considerably. Coma affects the image progressively less towards the centre, so keep bright highlights away from the frame corners if your lens suffers from the problem.

Astigmatism Astigmatism causes a lens to form a linear, rather than a circular, image of a point source of light–and the line changes from a vertical to a horizontal orientation as you focus the lens. Most modern lenses are well corrected for this fault, but residual astigmatism may result in vertical lines in the subject appearing sharper than horizontal ones. Again, stopping down improves the picture.

Diffraction Most lens aberrations become less noticeable at smaller apertures. Diffraction, however, does the opposite, blurring the whole image equally. This puts a limit on how far you can profitably stop a lens down and it is a good argument for testing lenses. A methodical test will reveal the optimum aperture at which other aberrations are miminized, while diffraction is still contained at an acceptable level.

Distortion Barrel and pincushion distortions are perhaps the most obvious of all lens aberrations and they are found only in non-symmetrical designs. In extreme examples, a zoom lens may bow parallel lines away from the frame centre at the wide-angle setting, and toward the centre when set to telephoto. With fixed focal length lenses, try to ensure that there are no straight lines parallel and close to the frame edges; which you can then use when control of distortion is a priority.

Lens fault	Corners worse than middle?	Longer focal length	Greater subject distance	Improved by stopping down?
Curvature of field	Yes	Improves	Improves	Yes
Axial chromatic aberration	No	No change	No change	Yes
Transverse chromatic aberration	No	Worsens	No change	No
Spherical abberation	Yes	Improves	Improves	Yes
Coma	Yes	Improves	No change	Yes
Astigmatism	Yes	Improves	No change	Yes
Diffraction	No	No change	No change	Gets worse
Distortion	Yes	No change	No change	No

6 Lighting and exposure data

Table 6.1 The Electromagnetic Spectrum

Frequency (Hz)	Wavelength (nm)	Type of Radiation
10^{2}	10^{16}	Long radio waves
10^{3} (kHz)	10^{15}	"
10^{4}	10^{14}	"
10^{5}	10^{13}	AM radio
10^{6} (MHz)	10^{12} (1 km)	"
10^{7}	10^{11}	FM radio & television
10^{8}	10^{10}	"
10^{9}	10^{9} (1 m)	Short radio waves
10^{10}	10^{8}	"
10^{11}	10^{7} (1 cm)	Microwaves
10^{12}	10^{6} (1mm)	"
10^{13}	10^{5}	Infra-red radiation
10^{14}	10^{4}	"
10^{15}	10^{3} (1 μm)	"
10^{16}	10^{2}	Light (~400–700nm)
10^{17}	10	Ultraviolet radiation
10^{18}	1 nm	Soft x rays
10^{19}	0.1 (1Å)	Hard x rays
10^{20}	10^{-2}	Gamma rays
10^{21}	10^{-3}	"
10^{22}	10^{-4}	"
10^{23}	10^{-5}	"

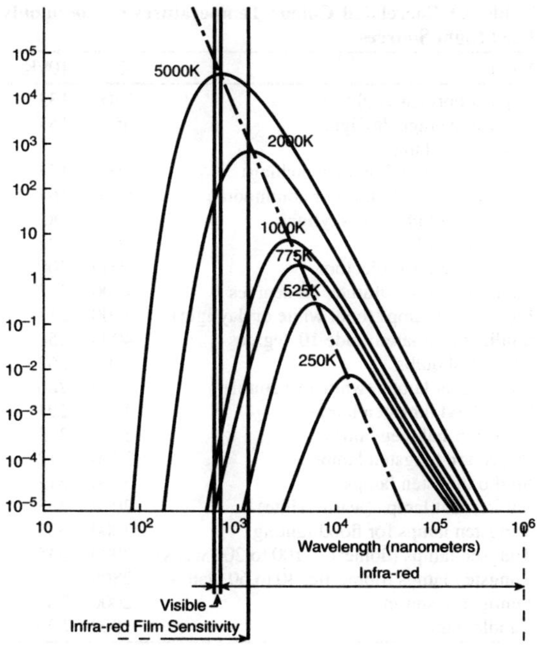

Figure 6.2 Infra-red sources. Blackbody emissions at different temperatures, measured on the Kelvin scale. K = degrees Celcius (°C) + 273. (Reprinted courtesy of Eastman Kodak Company.)

Table 6.3 Correlated Colour Temperatures of Commonly Used Light Sources

Source	K	10^6/K
Typical north skylight	7500	133
Typical average daylight	6500	154
Fluorescent lamps		
(northlight or Colour-matching)	6500	154
Xenon (electronic flash or continuous)	6000	167
Typical sunlight plus skylight	5500	182
Blue flash bulbs	5500	182
Carbon arc for projectors	5000	200
Sunlight at solar altitude 20 degrees	4700	213
Fluorescent lamps (cool white or daylight)	4300	233
Sunlight at solar altitude 10 degrees	4000	250
Clear flashbulbs	3800	263
Fluorescent lamps (white or natural)	3500	286
Photoflood tungsten lamps	3400	294
Tungsten-halogen lamps	3300	303
Projection tungsten lamps	3200	312
Studio tungsten lamps	3200	312
Fluorescent lamps (warm white)	3000	333
Tungsten lamps for floodlighting	3000	333
Tungsen lamps (domestic, 100 to 200 watts)	2900	345
Tungsten lamps (domestic, 40 to 60 watts)	2800	357
Sunlight at sunset	2000	500
Candle flame	1900	526

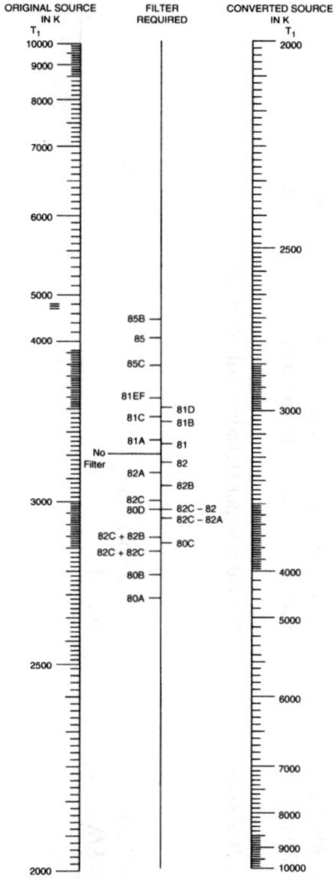

Figure 6.4 Nomograph for light source conversion

Table 6.5 Photometric Quantities: Symbols, Defining Equations, Units, and Abbreviations

Quantity	Symbol	Defining Equations	SI Unit	Abbreviation
Luminous flux	Φ_v	$\Phi = dQ/dt$	Lumen	lm
Lminous exitance	M_v	$M = d\Phi/dA$	Lumen per square metre	lm/m^2
Illuminance	E_v	$E = d\Phi/dA$	Lux (lumen per square metre)	lx
Luminous intensity (formerly candlepower)	I_v	$I = d\Phi/d_\omega$	Candela (lumen per steradian)	cd
Luminance (formerly photometric brightness)	L_v	$L = dI/d(A\cos\theta)$	Nit (lumen per steradian square metre)	
Source efficacy and efficiency definitions:				
Luminous efficacy	K	$K = \Phi_v/\Phi_e$	Lumen per watt	lm/W
Luminous efficiency	η	$\eta = K/K_{max}$	[ratio]	

Table 6.6 Conversion Factors for Luminance Units

	Nit	Stilb	Apostilb	Lambert	Millilambert	Footlambert	Candela/ft^2
1 nit	1.0	$1.0 \cdot 10^{-4}$	π	$\pi \cdot 10^{-4}$	$\pi \cdot 10^{-1}$	$2.92 \cdot 10^{-1}$	$9.29 \cdot 10^{-2}$
1 stilb	$1.0 \cdot 10^{4}$	1.0	$\pi \cdot 10^{4}$	π	$\pi \cdot 10^{3}$	$2.92 \cdot 10^{3}$	$9.29 \cdot 10^{2}$
1 apostilb	$1/\pi$	$1/\pi \cdot 10^{-4}$	1.0	$1.0 \cdot 10^{4}$	$1.0 \cdot 10^{-1}$	$9.29 \cdot 10^{-2}$	$2.96 \cdot 10^{-2}$
1 lambert	$1/\pi \cdot 10^{4}$	$1/\pi$	$1.0 \cdot 10^{4}$	1.0	$1.0 \cdot 10^{3}$	$9.29 \cdot 10^{2}$	$2.96 \cdot 10^{2}$
1 millilambert	$1/\pi \cdot 10^{1}$	$1/\pi \cdot 10^{-3}$	$1.0 \cdot 10^{1}$	$1.0 \cdot 10^{-3}$	1.0	$9.29 \cdot 10^{-1}$	$2.96 \cdot 10^{-1}$
1 foot lambert	3.43	$3.43 \cdot 10^{-4}$	$1.08 \cdot 10^{1}$	$1.08 \cdot 10^{-3}$	1.08	1.0	$1/\pi$
1 candela/ft^2	$1.08 \cdot 10^{1}$	$1.08 \cdot 10^{-3}$	$3.38 \cdot 10^{1}$	$3.38 \cdot 10^{-3}$	3.38	π	1.0

Table 6.7 Luminous Efficacy of Typical Broadband Sources

15 W Tungsten bulb	10 lm/W
100 W Tungsten bulb	20 lm/W
Fluorescent bulb	75 lm/W
High pressure sodium	120 lm/W

Luninous efficiency (h) is the ratio of a given source's efficacy to the maximum (683 lm/W):

$$\text{Luminous efficiency} = \text{Efficacy}(\lambda)/\text{Efficacy}_{max} = \text{Efficacy}(\lambda)/683$$

Beeause the value represents a ratio of efficacies, it is dimensionless. Luminous efficiencies are often stated as percentages. For example, the luminous efficiency of a helium neon laser is Efficacy (632.8 nm)/Efficiacy_{max} = 169.4/683 = 0.2480, or 24.8%

Table 6.8 Radiometric Quantities, Defining Equations, and SI Units

Quantity	Symbol	Defining Equation	SI Unit	Abbreviation
Radiant flux	Φ_e	$\Phi = dQ/dt$	Watt	W
Radiant exitance (radiant emittance)	M_e	$M = d\Phi/dA$	Watt per square metre	W/m^2
Irradiance	E_e	$E = d\Phi/dA$	Watt per square metre	W/m^2
Radiant intensity	I_e	$I = d\Phi/d_\omega$	Watt per steradian	W/sr
Luminance	L_e	$L = dI/d(A\cos\theta)$	Watt per steradian square metre	W/sr m^2

Table 6.9 International Standards Organisation (ISO) Film Speed Values

ISO (Arithmetic)	Log H_m	ISO° (Logarithmic)	ISO (Arithmetic)	Log H_m	ISO° (Logarithmic)
6	$\bar{1}.10$	9°	320	$\bar{3}.40$	26°
8	$\bar{1}.00$	10°	400	$\bar{3}.30$	27°
10	$\bar{2}.90$	11°	500	$\bar{3}.20$	28°
12	$\bar{2}.80$	12°	640	$\bar{3}.10$	29°
16	$\bar{2}.70$	13°	800	$\bar{3}.00$	30°
20	$\bar{2}.60$	14°	1000	$\bar{4}.90$	31°
25	$\bar{2}.50$	15°	1250	$\bar{4}.80$	32°
32	$\bar{2}.40$	16°	1600	$\bar{4}.70$	33°
40	$\bar{2}.30$	17°	2000	$\bar{4}.60$	34°
50	$\bar{2}.20$	18°	2500	$\bar{4}.50$	35°
64	$\bar{2}.10$	19°	3200	$\bar{4}.40$	36°
80	$\bar{2}.00$	20°	4000	$\bar{4}.30$	37°
100	$\bar{3}.90$	21°	5000	$\bar{4}.20$	38°
125	$\bar{3}.80$	22°	6400	$\bar{4}.10$	39°
160	$\bar{3}.70$	23°	8000	$\bar{4}.00$	40°
200	$\bar{3}.60$	24°	10,000	$\bar{5}.90$	41°
250	$\bar{3}.50$	25°	12,500	$\bar{5}.80$	42°

ISO Speed Values (arithmetic and logarithmic) and their corresponding log exposure values (H_m) for black-and-white films. Speed values are in increments of 1/3-stops. Logarithmic speed values are designated by the degree symbol (°).
(ISO film speed = $1/H_m \times 0.8$).

6.10 ISO Film speed Calculation

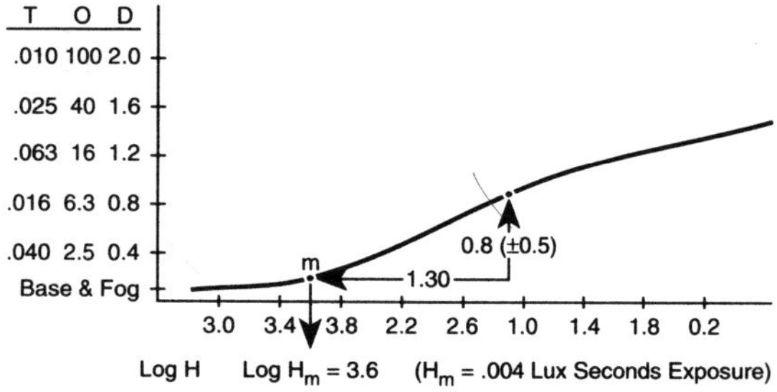

ISO Film Speed Calculation for black-and-white films.
ISO = $1/H_m \times 0.8 = 1/.004 \times 0.8 = 250 \times 0.8$
ISO = 200

Table 6.11 Transmittance (T), Reflectance (R), Opacity (O), and Density (D) Relationships

T(R)	O	D	T(R)	O	D	T(R)	O	D	T(R)	O	D	T(R)	O	D
0	∞	∞	.032	31	1.50	.170	5.9	.77	.410	2.44	.39	.720	1.39	.14
.001	1000	3.00	.034	29	1.47	.180	5.6	.74	.420	2.38	.38	.740	1.35	.13
.002	500	2.70	.036	28	1.44	.190	5.3	.72	.430	2.33	.37	.760	1.32	.12
.003	333	2.52	.038	26	1.42	.200	5.0	.70	.440	2.27	.36	.780	1.28	.11
.004	250	2.40	.040	25	1.40				.450	2.22	.35	.800	1.25	.10
.005	200	2.30				.210	4.8	.68	.460	2.17	.34			
.006	167	2.22	.045	22	1.35	.220	4.6	.66	.470	2.13	.33	.820	1.22	.09
.007	143	2.15	.050	20	1.30	.230	4.4	.64	.480	2.08	.32	.840	1.19	.08
.008	125	2.10	.055	18	1.26	.240	4.2	.62	.490	2.04	.31	.860	1.16	.07
.009	111	2.05	.060	17	1.22	.250	4.0	.60	.500	2.00	.30	.880	1.14	.06
.010	100	2.00	.065	15	1.19	.260	3.9	.58				.900	1.11	.05
			.070	14	1.15	.270	3.7	.57	.520	1.92	.28			
.011	91	1.96	.075	13	1.13	.280	3.6	.55	.540	1.85	.27	920	1.09	.04
.012	83	1.92	.080	12.5	1.10	.290	3.5	.54	.560	1.79	.25	.940	1.06	.03
.013	77	1.89	.085	12	1.07	.300	3.3	52	.580	1.72	.24	.960	1.04	.02
.014	71	1.85	.090	11	1.05				.600	1.67	.22	.980	1.02	.01
.015	67	1.82	.095	10.5	1.02	.310	3.2	.51				1.00	1.00	0
.016	62	1.80	.100	10	1.00	.320	3.1	.49	.620	1.61	.21			
.017	59	1.77				.330	3.0	.48	.640	1.56	.19			
.018	56	1.74	.105	9.5	.98	.340	2.9	.47	.660	1.52	.18			

Table 6.11 continued

T(R)	O	D	T(R)	O	D	T(R)	O	D	T(R)	O	D
.019	53	1.72	.110	9.1	.96	.350	2.86	.46	.680	1.47	.17
.020	50	1.70	.115	8.7	.94	.360	2.78	.44	.700	1.43	.15
			.120	8.3	.92	.370	2.70	.43			
.022	45	1.66	.125	8.0	.90	.380	2.63	.42			
.024	42	1.62	.130	7.7	.89	.390	2.56	.41			
.026	38	1.59	.135	7.4	.87	.400	2.50	.40			
.028	36	1.55	.140	7.1	.85						
.030	33	1.52	.145	6.9	.84						
			.150	6.7	.82						
			.155	6.5	.81						
			.160	6.3	.80						

Transmittance (T), *Reflectance* (R), *Opacity* (O), *and Density* (D)

$$\text{Transmittance or Reflectance} = \frac{\text{Light transmitted or reflected}}{\text{Incident light}}$$

Opacity = 1/T or 1/R
Density = log 1/T or log 1/R or log opacity
Example: If transmittance (or reflectance) is 0.50 (50%)
Density = log 1/0.50; = log 2; = 0.30

Table 6.12 Exponents, Factors, Logarithms, f-stops, Zones

Exponents	(Base 2) Factors	Log_2	Exponents	(Base 10) Factors	Log_{10}	*f*-stop change	Zone change
2^0	1	0	10^0	1	0	0	0
2^1	2	1	$10^{.3}$	2	.3	1	1
2^2	4	2	$10^{.6}$	4	.6	2	2
2^3	8	3	$10^{.9}$	8	.9	3	3
			($10^{1.0}$	10	1.0)		
2^4	16	4	$10^{1.2}$	16	1.2	4	4
2^5	32	5	$10^{1.5}$	32	1.5	5	5
2^6	64	6	$10^{1.8}$	64	1.8	6	6
			($10^{2.0}$	100	2.0)		
2^7	128	7	$10^{2.1}$	128	2.1	7	7
2^8	256	8	$10^{2.4}$	256	2.4	8	8
2^9	512	9	$10^{2.7}$	512	2.7	9	9
2^{10}	1024	10	$10^{3.0}$	1000	3.0	10	10

Logarithms are exponents to some *base*, such as 2 or 10. Some variables in photography (and computer memory in bits and bytes) are based on exponents (logarithms) to the base 2. This means that as the exponents increase by one, the factor doubles. (Computer memory chips having 1024 bits, have 2^{10} bits.) (*continued over*)

In photography, all factors representing a doubling or halving of exposure, such as full *f*-stops, shutter speed settings, light values, exposure value numbers on most exposure meters, and zone numbers, are based on logarithms to the base 2. However, neutral density filters, density, and log H are based on logarithms to the base 10. As exponents to the base 10 increase by one, the factors increase 10 times. In practical terms, a 0.30 neutral density filter can be thought of as a 1-stop filter, a 0.60 filter as a 2-stop filter, and so on. A log exposure increase of 0.30 is a doubling of exposure. Further, each 0.10 log change in exposure is equivalent to ⅓rd of a stop.

An average outdoor scene has a brightness range of about 128 to 1 (factor), or 2^7, 7 *f*-stops, 7 zones, or a log luminance range of 2.1, which is $10^{2.1}$. Film has a log exposure (log H) range (latitude) of about 1000 to 1, or $10^{3.0}$. Photographic paper has a reflectance density range of about 2.0, a factor of 100 to 1 or 10^2. (Note: Exponents to base 10 have been rounded off for simplicity, more correctly $10^{.301} = 2$.)

6.13 Photographic Effects

The basic causes of effects given in this summary are those widely accepted and are indicated in the first column as follows: (1) Size of latent image specks, (2) Regression of latent image, (3) Latent image situation (on the surface or interior of the grains), (4) Development effects. The arrows indicate the direction of an effect, e.g., with low-intensity reciprocity failure the sensitivity decreases with decreasing illuminance (I) and increasing time (t). D* is the optical density of the developed image.

	1st Exposure		Intermediate	2nd Exposure			
Effect	I	t	treatment	I	t	Remarks	Result
Reciprocity failure: low illuminances (2)	Low	Long	–	–	–	D^* = constant	Sensitivity decrease
	←	→					←
high illuminances (1, 3)	High	Short	–	–	–	D^* = constant	Sensitivity decrease
	→	←					→
	V. High	V. short	–	–	–	No failure:	Sensitivity constant
	→	←					
Hypersensitization by pre-exposure (1)	High	Short	–	Low	Long	1st uniform	Sensitivity for 2nd exposure increased
	→	←		←	→	2nd camera	→
Latent-image intensification (1)	High	Short	–	Low	Long	1st camera	Sensitivity for 1st exposure increased
	→	←		←	→	2nd uniform	→

Table 6.13 continued

Effect	1st Exposure I	1st Exposure t	Intermediate treatment	2nd Exposure I	2nd Exposure t	Remarks	Result
Temperature:							
reduced (2)	Low ←	Long →	–	–	–	This represents a change in reciprocity failure	Sensitivity increase →
(1,3)	High →	Short ←	–	–	–		Sensitivity decrease ←
very low	Independent of illum.		–	–			Sensitivity always lower than optimum at room temperature
Increased	Low ←	Long →	–	–	–		Sensitivity decrease ←
	High →	Short ←	–	–	–		Sensitivity increase →
Intermittent exposures Schwarzchild effect	High →	Short ←	–	–	–	(Often)	Sensitivity increase →
	Low ←	Long →	–	–	–		Sensitivity decrease ←
High frequency	–	–	–	–	–	Result according to average intensity	
Solarization	Continued exposure		–	–		Only for surface image which is rebrominated	Reversal

Table 6.13 continued

Effect	1st Exposure I	t	Intermediate treatment	2nd Exposure I	t	Remarks	Result
Herschel: (3)							Bleaching or reversal of
visual	White light		–	Red light		–	print-out density
latent	White light		–	Red light		–	latent density
low temperature	At very low temp.		Keep cold	Red light		–	Very effective bleaching
			Warm up	Red light		–	No bleaching
Debot (3)	Heavy, to white light		Bleach surface image	Redlight		Surface image (converse of Herschel effect)	Red sensitivity
Dye reversal	White light		Dyeing	Light absorbed by dye		Only with certain dyes	Reversal
Seebeck	White light		–	Coloured light	–		Print-out image in colour of second exposure
Becquerel	White light		–	Yellow or red		Agl emulsions	Print-out positive image of second exposure
	White light		–	Yellow or red		Physical dev.	Developed positive image of second exposure

Table 6.13 continued

Effect	1st Exposure I	1st Exposure t	Intermediate treatment	2nd Exposure I	2nd Exposure t	Remarks	Result
	White light`		–	Yellow or red		Chemical dev.	Herschel reversal
Weigert	Uniform, white polarized		–	Polarized, coloured		According to wave-length	Dichroic print-out images
	Polarized		–	–		–	Dichroic developed density
Clayden (3)	V. high	V. short	–	Normal or low	Normal or long	Surface latent image	Desensitization towards second exposure
Very low temperature (3)	At very low temp		Warm up	Exposure to light		–	Desensitization towards second exposure
Villard (3)	X rays		–	Light		–	Desensitization towards second exposure
Pressure (3)	Pressure	–	–	–			Produces some latent image
	Pressure		–	Light		–	Desensitization towards second exposure

Table 6.13 continued

Effect	1st Exposure I	1st Exposure t	Intermediate treatment	2nd Exposure I	2nd Exposure t	Remarks	Result
Russell	Contact with metal and other substances			–	–	–	Produces latent image
	Contact with metal and other substances			–	Light	(Often)	Desensitization towards second exposure
Sterry	Light		Chromates	–		–	Lowering of contrast
Albert (3)	Stepped to light		Nitric acid	Uniform to light		Surface image	Reversed
Sabattier	Uniform to light		Partly developed	Stepped to light or Na_2HAsO_3		–	Reversal of 2nd exposure
Purkinje	Shift in maximum of *luminosity curve* with change in *luminous intensity*						
Kron	Shift of optimum of reciprocity failure curve towards high intensities with increasing time of development						
Ross	Contraction of small images due to tanning action of developer						
Capri-blue	Increase in sensitivity and contrast of coarse-grain emulsions without silver-sulphide sensitivity-specks by certain dyes						
Eberhard, Neighborhood, and Kostinsky	Value of a developed density depends on neighbouring density; produced by developer reaction products. Edge effects						
High-energy quanta or particles, as x-rays, protons, electrons	Straight line density-time characteristics, highest slope at origin; Same shape characteristics for all wave-engths;Absence of reciprocity failure. A single quantum or particle will form a latent-image speck						

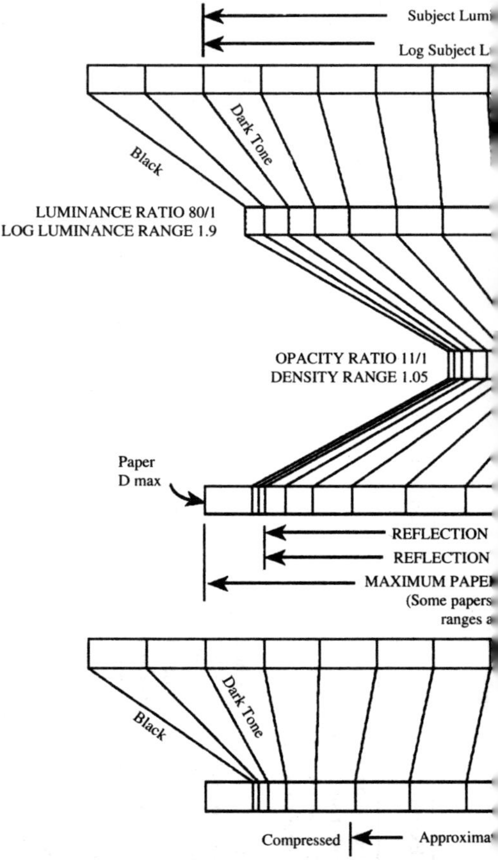

Graphical Representation of Typical Photographic Tone Reprodu

(Top)
SUBJECT: Represented in equal log luminance increments.
OPTICAL IMAGE: Compression in shadow areas due to flare.
NEGATIVE: Overall compression, but more in shadow areas.
PRINT: Compression in highlights and shadows. Midtones expa

(Bottom)
PRINT compared to SUBJECT: Compression of highlights and sl
Only slight contrast changes in midtone areas.
(Courtesy of the Eastman Kodak Company)

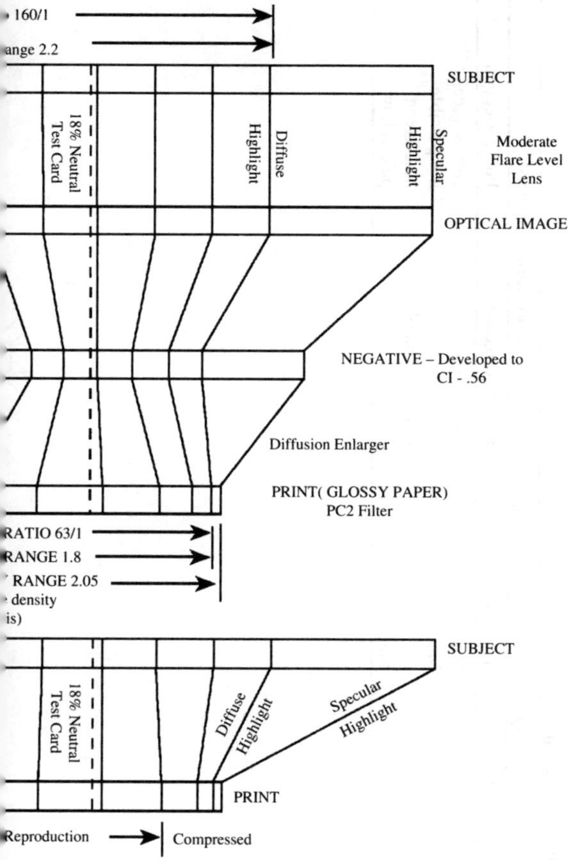

160/1
ange 2.2
SUBJECT
18% Neutral Test Card
Highlight
Diffuse
Highlight
Specular
Moderate Flare Level Lens
OPTICAL IMAGE
NEGATIVE – Developed to CI - .56
Diffusion Enlarger
PRINT(GLOSSY PAPER) PC2 Filter
RATIO 63/1
RANGE 1.8
RANGE 2.05
density
is)
SUBJECT
18% Neutral Test Card
Diffuse
Highlight
Specular
Highlight
PRINT
Reproduction
Compressed

Table 6.15 Correction filters for black-and-white photography

Light source	Film sensitization	Rendering of colours		Correction filter need	
		Too dark	Too light	Partial correction	Full correction
Daylight	pan	green	blue	pale yellow	yellow-green
Daylight	ortho	red	blue	pale yellow	not possible
Tungsten	pan	blue	red	pale greenish blue	blue-green
Electronic flash	pan	–	blue	–	pale yellow

Table 6.16 Contrast filters for black-and-white photography

Filter	Colour	Absorbs	Lightens	Typical uses
Tricolour blue	blue	red, green	blue	copying, emphasis of haze
Tricolour green	green	blue, red	green	landscape photography
Tricolour red	red	blue, green	red	cloud photography, haze penetration
Narrow-band blue	deep blue	red, green, some blue	blue	
Narrow-band green	deep green	blue, red, some green	green	copying and colour separation
Narrow-band red	deep red	blue, green, some red	red	
Minus-blue	yellow	blue	yellow	cloud photography
Minus-green	magenta	green	magenta	copying
Minus-red	cyan	red	cyan	copying
Orange ('furniture red')	deep orange	blue, some green	red	emphasis of wood grain

Table 6.17 Light-balancing and colour-conversion filters for use with colour films.
Type A is balanced for articial light of 3400K (photoflood); Type B is balanced for artificial light of 3200K (studio lamp); Type D is balanced for daylight of 5500 K.

Filter colour	Mired shift value	Exposure increase in stops	Typical use
	–81	1	Type D film with aluminium flashbulbs
	–56	⅔	Type D film with zirconium flashbulbs
Pale blue	–45	⅔	Type B film with GS lamps
	–32	⅓	Type B film with GS lamps
	–18	⅓	Type A film with 3200 K lighting
	–10	⅓	
	+10	⅓	With electronic flash
	+18	⅓	Type B film with photofloods
Pale amber	+27	⅓	
	+35	⅓	Type A or B film with clear flashbulbs
	+53	⅔	
	+112	⅔	Type A films in daylight
Salmon-pink	+130	⅔	Type B films in daylight
Blue	–130	2	Type D films in 3200 K lighting

6.18 Filtering other light sources

If a scene is lit by a mixture of fluorescent and other lights, a better approach may be to leave the tubes unfiltered and place gels over the other lamps. For example, you may wish to put green gels on windows to balance the colour of daylight with that of the fluorescents; a magenta filter over the camera lens then corrects the hue of both fluorescents and windows. If you are using flash, this technique is very economical, since you can use small pieces of filter gel over the flash unit.

Both Rosco and Lee manufacture filters of this type, but there is no common standard; the manufacturers' catalogues provide full details.

Filtration and additional exposure (stops)

Lamp type	Tungsten balanced		Daylight balanced	
US tubes				
Daylight	85B + 40M + 30Y	+ 1⅔	50M + 50Y	+1⅓
White	60M + 50Y	+ 1⅔	30M + 20C	+1
Warm white	50M + 40Y	+1	40M + 40C	+1
Warm white deluxe	10M + 10Y	+⅔	30M + 60C	+2
Cool white	60R	+1⅓	40M + 10Y	+1
Cool white deluxe	50M + 50Y	+1⅓	20M + 30C	+⅔

UK tubes

Lamp	Tungsten film		Daylight film	
Daylight	85B + 30M + 10Y	+1⅔	40M + 30Y	+1
White	40M + 40Y	+1	20C + 30M	+1
Warm white	30M + 20Y	+1	40C + 40M	+1⅓
Warm white deluxe	10Y	+⅓	60C + 30M	+1⅔
Cool white	50M + 60Y	+1⅓	30M	+⅔
Cool white deluxe	10M + 30Y	+⅔	30C + 20M	+1
Natural/ Colourite	–	–	10R	+⅓
Northlight and artificial daylight	–		85	+⅔
Unidentified	30M	+⅔	50M + 50Y	+1⅓

"Impossible" corrections

All cool (i.e. non-incandescent) light sources produce a discontinous spectrum, as shown below. Some sources, though, are better than others, and electronic flash, for example, matches daylight perfectly. However, the worst light sources of this type totally lack certain wavelengths, and no amount of filtration will provide a good colour result. The best approach is to light the scene with tungsten or flash, and briefly switch on those light sources that actually appear in the pictures so that they appear illuminated on film. Where this is impossible, use the corrections below –but be prepared for a heavy colour cast.

Filtration and exposure compensation (stops)

Lamp type	Tungsten balanced		Daylight balanced	
High-pressure sodium	50M + 20C	+1	80B + 20C	+2⅓
Metal halide	60R + 20Y	+1⅔	40M + 20Y	+1
Deluxe white mercury	70R + 10Y	+1⅔	60M + 30Y	+1
Clear mercury	90R + 40Y	+2	50R + 20M + 20Y	+1⅓

Colour compensating filters

These filter factors (in stops) are nominal, and they should be checked for critical work.

Units of filtration

Colour	05	10	20	30	40	50
Cyan	⅓	⅓	⅓	⅔	⅔	1
Magenta	⅓	⅓	⅓	⅔	⅔	⅔
Yellow	0	⅓	⅓	⅓	⅓	⅔
Red	⅓	⅓	⅓	⅔	⅔	1
Green	⅓	⅓	⅓	⅔	⅔	1
Blue	⅓	⅓	⅔	⅔	⅔	1⅓

If you have a complete set of the subtractive colours, you can use it to make up additive primaries–20R = 20M + 20Y, 20G = 20Y + 20C, and 20B = 20M + 20C. However, remember that you should never have filters of all three subtractive colours in use at once, because this simply adds neutral density. Remove equal amounts of all colours until just two filters are in use.

Table 6.19 Properties of photocells used in exposure determination systems

Photocell type	Se	CdS	SPD	GPD
Battery needed	No	Yes	Yes	Yes
Amplifier needed	No	No	Yes	Yes
Speed of response	Slow	Slow	Fast	Very fast
Memory effects	Eventually	Yes	No	No
Sensitivity	Low	Medium to high	High to very high	High
Linear response	Approximately	Poor	Yes	Yes
Spectral (colour) sensitivity	Matches eye	Red bias	Needs blue filter	No infrared sensitivity
Size	Large	Small	Small	Small
Range change device needed	Yes	Yes	No	No
Electrical property	Photovoltaic	Photoconductor or photoresistor	Photovoltaic	Photovoltaic
Cost of unit	Medium	Low	High	High

Table 6.20 The properties of some light sources used in photography

Source	Type of spectrum: C. continuous L. line B. line plus continuum	Colour temperature (kelvins)	Efficacy (lumens per watt)	Average lamp life (hours)	Light output H. high M. moderate L. low	Constancy of output P. poor G. good E. excellent V. variable	Costs: L. low M. moderate H. high — Initial	Costs: Running	Size of unit: S. small M. medium L. large	Ease of operation: D. difficult M. moderate S. simple
Daylight	C	2000–20000			H–L	P		L		S
Tungsten filament lamps:										
General service	C	2760–2960	†13	1000	L	P	L	L	M	S
Photographic	C	3200	†20	100	L	G	M	M	M	S
Photoflood	C	3400	†40	3–10	M	P	L	M	S	S
Projector	C	3200	†20	25–100	M	G	M	M	S	S
Tungsten halogen lamps	C	2700–3400	15–35	25–200	M	E	M	H	S,M	S
Carbon arc lamps:										
Low intensity	C	3800–10 000		1–2	H	P	H	L	L	D
High intensity	C	6000		1–2	H	P	H	L	L	D
White flame	C	5000		1–2	H	P	H	L	L	D
Mercury vapour discharge lamps:										
Low pressure	L		6		M	G	H	L	M	S

Table 6.20 continued

Source	Type of spectrum: C. continous L. line B. line plus continuum	Colour temperature (kelvins)	Efficacy (lumens per watt)	Average lamp life (hours)	Light output H. high M. moderate L. low	Constancy of output P. poor G. good E. excellent V. variable	Costs: L. low M. moderate H. high		Size of unit: S. small M. medium L. large	Ease of operation: D. difficult M. moderate S. simple
							Initial	Running		
High pressure	L		35–55	1000–2000	H	G	H	L	M	S
Fluorescent lamps	B	*3000–6500	†62	7000–8000	M	P	M	L	L	M
Sodium vapour discharge lamps:										
Low pressure	L		170	10–16 000	H	E	M	L	M	M
High pressure	L		100		H	E	H	L	M	M
Metal halide lamps	B	5600–6000	85–100	200–1000	H	E,V	H	H	M	M
Pulsed xenon lamps	B	5600	25–50	300–1000	H	G	H	L	M,S	M
Flash bulbs	C	3800 or 5500		used once only	H	E	L	H	S	S
Electronic flash	B	*6000	40		M	G	H,M,L	L	L,M,S	M

*correlated value
†typical value

Table 6.21 Photometric units and camera exposure

Approximate corresponding values of various units of luminance and illuminance related to exposure value (EV) for camera exposure determination with a film of speed ISO 100/21°

	Subject luminance (brightness)						Illuminance (illumination on subject)			
EV (for ISO 100/21°)	cd/m^2 (nit)	stilb cd/cm^2 (sb)	apostilb lm/m^2 (asb)	cd/ft^2	lambert (L)	foot-lambert (ft L)	lux lm/m^2 (lx)	phot lm/cm^2	lm/ft^2	EV (for ISO 100/21° and R = 1)
–2	0.03		0.1			0.01	0.1		0.01	–2
–1	0.06		0.2			0.02	0.2		0.02	–1
0	0.13		0.4	0.01		0.04	0.4		0.04	0
1	0.25		0.8	0.02		0.07	0.8		0.07	1
2	0.5		1.6	0.05		0.15	1.6		0.15	2
3	1		3.14	0.09		0.29	3.1		0.29	3
4	2		6.28	0.2		0.58	6.3		0.58	4
5	4		12.57	0.4		1.17	12.6		1.2	5
6	8	0.001	25.1	0.8		2.34	25		2.3	6
7	16	0.002	50.3	1.5		4.67	50		4.7	7
8	32	0.003	100.5	3	0.01	9.34	100	0.01	9	8
9	64	0.006	201	6	0.02	18.7	201	0.02	19	9
10	128	0.01	402	12	0.04	37.5	402	0.04	37	10
11	256	0.03	804	24	0.08	75	804	0.08	75	11

Table 6.21 continued

	Subject luminance (brightness)						Illuminance (illumination on subject)			
EV (for ISO 100/21°)	cd/m^2 (nit)	stilb cd/cm^2 (sb)	apostilb lm/m^2 (asb)	cd/ft^2	lambert (L)	foot-lambert (ft L)	lux lm/m^2 (lx)	phot lm/cm^2	lm/ft^2	EV (for ISO 100/21° and R = 1)
12	512	0.05	1609	48	0.16	150	1609	0.16	150	12
13	1024	0.1	3217	96	0.32	299	3217	0.32	299	13
14	2048	0.21	6434	190	0.64	598	6434	0.64	598	14
15	4096	0.41	12868	381	1.29	1196	12868	1.29	1196	15
16	8192	0.82	25736	761	2.57	2392	25736	2.57	2392	16
17	16384	1.64	51472	1522	5.15	4784	51472	5.15	4784	17
18	32768	3.23	102944	3044	10.29	9568	102944	10.29	9568	18

6.22 Camera exposure

Introduction

Most modern cameras set exposure automatically, but there are times when it is useful to be able to estimate the correct exposure without referring to a meter. At night, for example, your camera's meter may not respond to low levels of light or it may give a misleading reading. Even in brightly lit conditions, an intuitive feeling for exposure ensures that you notice when your meter malfunctions.

Sources of exposure error

The commonest metering problem leading to incorrect exposure is "subject failure"–where the metered area is considerably darker or lighter than the scene as a whole. An incident light meter reading gets around this problem, but with a reflected light reading, experience and a working knowledge of the meter usually hold the key. Metering light reflected from a grey card (see below) eliminates subject failure, but an equally effective technique is to meter from the subject itself. You must then compensate by giving either increased or reduced exposure to take account of the non-standard subject reflectance.

Subject type	Adjust meter reading by
Sunlit snow, fresh white paintwork, clean white fabric	+ 2 stops
White sand, pale fabrics, weathered white paintwork, new plaster, pale grey sky	+1 stop
Weathered wood, light-coloured brickwork, green grass, dark grey or blue sky	No adjustment
Dark timber, freshly turned soil, autumn leaves, dark green foliage, blue sky deepened by polarizer	–1 stop
Dark coniferous woodland, dark suiting fabric	–2 stops
Matte black fabric	–3 stops

Other sources of error include:

Meter calibration The built-in meters found in the majority of modern cameras are calibrated to give good results with colour negative film, which benefits from a degree of overexposure. If you routinely use transparency film, this deliberate overexposure may produce unacceptable results. With any new camera, it is prudent to run an exposure test to calibrate the meter. Based on this; you may choose to set an exposure index up to a stop faster than the film's nominal ISO rating.

Zoom lenses Many zoom lenses have variable apertures: the aperture is smaller at the longer focal length settings. Contrary to widely held opinion, the error occurs throughout the aperture range, not just at full aperture, and it can be as much as one stop. TTL meters take the change into account, but don't forget to make the necessary correction when using flash or a separate hand-held meter.

Bright colours The colour sensitivity of a camera's meter may not match that of the film, or of your eye. Brilliant colours are especially misleading, so if you are photographing these types of coloured subjects, use a grey card or incident light meter reading. When you are using brilliantly coloured filters, first take the meter reading without the filter and then apply the manufacturer's filter factor.

Memory effect Certain types of meter cell–notably cadmium sulphide–have a "memory" that can lead to errors of up to a stop. To avoid this problem, give this type of meter a minute or two to adjust to a dramatic drop in brightness levels. In the reverse situation, direct the meter at a subject about one stop brighter before taking a reading.

Tungsten light Note that film speeds for monochrome materials are quoted for daylight. Tungsten light has a lower actinic quality and film speed is therefore lower. With panchromatic film, divide your film speed by 1.5; ortho films need a stop extra exposure, and blue-sensitive films, two.

Fluorescent light Alternating current causes fluorescent lights to flash at a pace that matches mains frequency. The flickering is too fast for the eye to see but it can cause metering errors with some first-generation electronic cameras. With focal plane shutters, the flickering also causes unevenness of exposure, so always use shutter speeds of 1/30 or slower when taking pictures by fluorescent light sources.

Exposure estimates

Bright sunlight is remarkably consistent in intensity at moderate latitudes, and you can use this fact to your advantage by estimating exposure using the "Sunny-16" rule. If you set the camera's aperture to f/16, the correct shutter speed is roughly equal to the film speed. As an example, if you are using ISO 400 film, you should set 1/400 at f/16–on most cameras 1/500 is the nearest equivalent.

This rule applies to front-lit subjects–for backlighting, give two stops additional exposure, and for sidelighting, one stop extra. Where surroundings are extremely bright, as on a beach of light sand or on snow, give one to two stops less exposure than the Sunny-16 rule indicates. In dimmer conditions, you will need to give extra exposure. In hazy sun, allow one extra stop; light cloud, two stops; and heavy overcast, three stops.

Bracketing and exposure latitude

Bracketing is an insurance policy that is familiar to most experienced photographers. However, bracketing intervals are most often dictated by habit, whereas they should ideally be matched to the film's exposure latitude and the lighting contrast. On a dull day with colour negative film, for example, bracketing at 1-stop intervals provides ample security. However sidelighting in sunny weather stretches the latitude of reversal film to the limit, and bracketing at 1/3-stop intervals is reasonable.

Grey card metering

If you don't have access to an incident light meter, a reflected light meter reading from the surface of an 18 per cent grey card makes a good substitute. Kodak supplies a standard grey card, but there are numerous widely available alternatives. The subject matter marked "no adjustment" in the chart on page 160 also makes a good substitute for a standard card.

The reverse of the standard grey card reflects 90 per cent of the incident light, and it therefore makes a useful highlight reference tone.

Problem exposures

Low light and extremely high-contrast subjects are notoriously difficult to meter, due to the fact that often the subject consists of brilliant highlights and pools of impenetrable shadow. In these circumstances exposure "guesses" ironically often produce better results than all but the most methodical metering. The two charts on pages 163 and 164 provide exposure information for difficult subjects.

In the left-hand column of the first table, you will find a range of different lighting conditions, and from these you can read off the correct exposure value for the film you are using. In the second chart, each diagonal bar represents a single exposure value, and by picking any point on the bar you can read up and across to find an appropriate shutter speed and aperture at the corresponding points on the horizontal and vertical axes.

For example, if you were photographing a floodlit sports event on ISO 800 film, the correct exposure value from chart 1 is 11. From chart 2, you will see that a range of shutter speeds and apertures give the correct exposure from 1/1000 at f/1.4 to 1 second at f/64. Obviously you would choose a fast shutter speed in this situation, but in others, long exposures from the upper end of the tinted bar might be more appropriate: if, for example, you were photographing headlight trails from moving vehicles, you would clearly need to set an exposure of ten seconds or more. Note that the recommended exposures don't take account of reciprocity failure.

Subject matter	Film speed (ISO) 64–100	125–200	250–400	400–800	1000–1600
Cityscape at night	1	2	3	4	5
Cityscape immediately after sunset	10	11	12	13	14
Cityscape at twilight	8	9	10	11	12
Moving vehicles on busy roads	3	4	5	6	7
Buildings lit up by flood lights	4	5	6	7	8
Festive illuminations outdoors	7	8	9	10	11
Neon advertising signs	9	10	11	12	13
Bright city streets– general view	7	8	9	10	11
Figure lit by street lights	4	5	6	7	8
Illuminated shop window displays	8	9	10	11	12
Bonfires–general view	8	9	10	11	12
Subjects lit by them	5	6	7	8	9
Firework displays– ground pieces	8	9	10	11	12
air bursts	9	10	11	12	13
Fairgrounds	6	7	8	9	10
Landscape by moonlight	–3	–2	–1	0	1
The moon itself–full	14	15	16	17	18
crescent	12	13	14	15	16
Partial eclipse of the sun, **using 5.0 ND filter**	13	14	15	16	17
Floodlit sports event at night	8	9	10	11	12
Circuses, theatre performances– general view	7	8	9	10	11
spotlit acts	9	10	11	12	13
School plays, amateur drama	5	6	7	8	9
Indoor sports–well lit	8	9	10	11	12
Swimming pools	6	7	8	9	10
Domestic interiors– general view	5	6	7	8	9
close to bright lights	6	7	8	9	10
candlelight	5	6	7	8	9
festive lights and Xmas trees	4	5	6	7	8
Hospitals–wards & maternity units	7	8	9	10	11
Churches & chapels– indoors by day	5	6	7	8	9
Public buildings and offices	8	9	10	11	12
Museums and galleries	5	6	7	8	9

Exposure values at ISO 100

	Shutter speed (1/secs)											Full seconds							
f/	2K	1K	500	250	125	60	30	15	8	4	2	1s	2s	4s	8s	15s	30s	1m	2 m
64	23	22	21	20	19	18	17	16	15	14	13	12	11	10	9	8	7	6	5
45	22	·	·	·	·	·	·	·	·	·	·	·	·	·	·	·	·	·	4
32	21	·	·	·	·	·	·	·	·	·	·	·	·	·	·	·	·	·	3
22	20	·	·	·	·	·	·	·	·	·	·	·	·	·	·	·	·	·	2
16	19	·	·	·	·	·	·	·	·	·	·	·	·	·	·	·	·	·	1
11	18	·	·	·	·	·	·	·	·	·	·	·	·	·	·	·	·	·	0
8	17	·	·	·	·	·	·	·	·	·	·	·	·	·	·	·	·	·	– 1
5.6	16	·	·	·	·	·	·	·	·	·	·	·	·	·	·	·	·	·	– 2
4	15	·	·	·	·	·	·	·	·	·	·	·	·	·	·	·	·	·	– 3
2.8	14	·	·	·	·	·	·	·	·	·	·	·	·	·	·	·	·	·	– 4
2	13	·	·	·	·	·	·	·	·	·	·	·	·	·	·	·	·	·	– 5
1.4	12	11	10	9	8	7	6	5	4	3	2	1	0	–1	–2	–3	–4	–5	– 6
f/	2K	1K	500	250	125	60	30	15	8	4	2	1s	2s	4s	8s	15s	30s	1m	2 m

Low light

Photography in low light presents special problems. The principal difficulty is the self-evident one of getting enough light onto the film, which is complicated by the fact that the film's sensitivity to light drops in dim conditions. This is the phenomenon known as reciprocity failure, or reciprocity law failure as it is sometimes called. Here is a pragmatic, practical guide–for a theoretical analysis, turn to virtually any serious photographic work on exposure.

The best way to cope with reciprocity failure is to avoid it. Sadly, this isn't always possible, because certain photographic applications actually demand long exposures. When using small apertures, you can sometimes avoid the problem by adding extra light, but to blur moving water, for example, you have no choice but to use an exposure of several seconds.

Reciprocity failure affects contrast as well as colour: in a scene that has a wide range of brightness levels, contrast increases still further at long exposure times. With monochrome film, you can compensate by cutting development; with colour, however, there is no such easy solution. Another aspect of the same problem is that when combining flash and (dim) available light, you must remember to compensate for reciprocity failure only when calculating exposure for those areas that are not lit by flash.

Data for the correction of reciprocity failure has two components–exposure and filtration. With colour film, it is safest to give the extra exposure by opening up the lens aperture. Leaving the shutter open longer has a less predictable effect, because the intensity of the light striking the film is unchanged. With monochrome you have more choice (see below). The exposure-compensation figure supplied always takes account of the density of any corrective filtration–don't allow additional exposure because of the filters.

The characteristics of each emulsion layer put an upper time limit on the degree of compensation for reciprocity failure. If you are forced to cross the barrier into the "Not Recommended" region of a film manufacturer's data, your pictures will probably shows signs of crossed characteristic curves. This means that shadows and highlights develop casts of different colours, with the result that no filtration will produce a satisfactory image.

If you regularly use automatic exposure control in dim light, bear in mind that exposure meters do not take account of film's reciprocity failure characteristics. This makes automatic exposure at shutter speeds longer than a second effectively useless.

Unknown emulsions Filtration and exposure compensations vary so widely between film that no general guidelines about corrections will be satisfactory in every case. However, averaging figures for exposure compensation produces this result:

Film type	1 second	10 seconds	100 seconds
Colour negative	+1 stop	+2 stops	+2½ stops
Colour reversal	+½ stops	+1½ stops	+2½ stops

If you can't locate up-to-date information about the film you are using, apply these corrections and bracket a stop either side to be safe.

Monochrome films Black and white film has such wide exposure latitude that reciprocity failure is less often a problem. However, when exposures exceed a second you should use the following corrections.

Indicated exposure	Use instead	Or open aperture	Cut development
1 sec	2 sec	1 stop	10%
10 sec	1 min	2 stops	20%
100 sec	20 min	3 stops	30%

Tungsten-balanced films In dim conditions, films balanced for tungsten light are generally a better choice than daylight-balanced emulsions. For this reason, if you frequently use long exposures in daylight illumination you may prefer to load a tungsten film into the camera and correct colour with an 80A filter.

Too dim to meter?

If you have difficulty getting a meter reading from the subject itself in dim light, try instead of taking a reflected light reading from a white card–then give two stops extra exposure. If even this doesn't work, point a reflected light meter toward the light source, take a reading and then open up five stops.

Bright lights

Film loses its speed at very short exposures, too. However, there are just two common situations where high-intensity reciprocity failure is likely to be noticeable. One is when you are using an electronic flashgun that delivers exposures shorter than 1/5000 at close subject distances. This may sometimes cause underexposure and a slight blue cast to be noticeable. The solution here is to use a CC05 or 10 yellow filter. High-intensity reciprocity failure also cause trouble when you are using tungsten films with fast shutter speeds or flash. Reciprocity failure may set in at speeds as slow as 1/60. Manufacturers don't supply filter and exposure recommendations for such eventualities, but the problem is generally easy to avoid in the majority of situations.

Judging exposure in dim light With experience you can use the threshold of vision to determine exposure. The technique works best with view cameras, but you could adapt it for smaller format cameras, too, provided that you exclude all extraneous light. To do this put your head under the focusing cloth and allow two or three minutes for your eyes to accommodate the light levels. Then gradually stop down the lens and judge the smallest aperture at which you can still see the shadow detail.

Smallest aperture at which shadow detail is seen	f/8	f/11	f/16	f/22	f/32	f/45	f/64
Exposure time at f/11 (ISO 100, secs)	64	32	16	8	4	2	1

This works only in dim lighting conditions; in sunlight it is possible to see some detail in even the deepest shadow areas of your subject.

6.23 Photographing TV, video and computer screens

The principal problem in photographing any video display is that the image is renewed line by line, which means that if you use fast shutter speeds you will record only a portion of the picture. The scan rate determines the fastest practical shutter speed, and this varies according to the TV standard in use. Most European countries use either PAL or SECAM, which both have scan rates of 50 cycles. In the USA and Japan, however, the TV system is NTSC, which has a slightly higher scan rate of 60 cycles.

Each system takes two scans to build up a whole picture, so the fastest shutter speeds you can use are 1/25 for PAL and SECAM, and 1/30 for NTSC. Faster speeds leave a dark bar across the screen and with slower speeds there is the risk of image movement spoiling the picture. The situation is complicated in Europe by the fact that few shutters have a speed of 1/25, and in America by the risk of the shutter running slightly fast and thus creating a dark bar. A handful of cameras have a "TV" exposure mode that is set to match exactly the TV scan rate. With other models it is best to use a speed of 1/15 to be sure of photographing a full picture.

If you want just the TV screen in the picture, darken the room, and check for extraneous reflections with the TV switched off. Switch on, tune in the best picture possible and then reduce the contrast slightly. TTL metres usually give a correct indication of exposure. For optimum colour results shoot a test roll, and mark or tape the TV control positions. NTSC sets have a hue control to allow you to adjust colour, but with PAL and SECAM the hues are fixed on broadcast, so you can fine tune hue only with filters.

If you need to include the TV in a wider picture, you should ideally make two exposures on a single frame: the first one records the screen in a darkened room; in the second, light the room and cover the screen in black cloth. As a precaution, before striking the set or leaving the location, it is wise to take these two shots on separate pieces of film, but his time, for the second, uncover the TV set and switch it off so that the edges of the tube pick up reflections of the room lighting. If all else fails, a retoucher can then combine the two images.

If you haven't time for all this, adjust room lighting to give a shutter speed of 1/15 and adjust the TV brightness to match the room. A video cassette recorder with a still-frame facility makes it easier for you to catch a particular image off the TV, but it may create noise bars.

To photograph computer screen images, follow the same rules, but because the picture is generally static, you can set a slower shutter speed – ¼ is a good choice. With liquid crystal displays you will obtain the best screen results by using a hard light source, such as a spotlight.

Remember that copyright exists on most TV images.

Table 7.1 Enlarger Size Categories

	Maximum Film Size[a]	Acceptable Smaller Film Formats[b]
Small format	35 mm (24 × 36 mm)	Subminiature (8 × 10 mm), 110 (13 × 17 mm), half frame 35 (18 × 24 mm), 126 (26.5 × 26.5 mm)
Medium format	6 × 9 (2¼ × 3¼ in.)	Full frame 35 (24 × 36 mm), 127 (4 × 4 cm), 645 (1⅝ × 2¼ in.), 6 × 6 (2¼ × 2¼ in.), 6 × 7 (2¼ × 2¾ in.)
Large format	4 × 5 in. (10 × 13 cm)	All in medium format plus 6 × 12 (2¼ × 4½ in.), 9 × 12 cm (3½ × 4½ in.)
Extra-large format	8 × 10 in. (20 × 25 cm)	4 × 5 in. (10 × 13 cm), 6 × 17 cm. (2¼ × 6⅝ in.), 5 × 5 in. (13 × 13 cm), 5 × 7 in. (13 × 18 cm). 9 × 9 in. (23 × 23 cm)

[a]All sizes listed by most common designation followed by closest alternative dimensions in parethensis.
[b]Other formats may be accommodated with accessories or with restrictions on system performance.

Table 7.2 Lens Selection Chart

Lens	Maximum Film Size[a]	Acceptable Film	Smaller Formats[b]
28 mm	Half frame 35 mm	Subminiature, 110	
50 mm	Full frame 35 mm	126	
80 mm	6 × 6 cm	645,127	
100 mm	6 × 9 cm	6 × 7 cm	
135 mm	6 × 12 cm	6 × 9 cm	
150 mm	4 × 5 in.	9 × 12 cm	
180 mm	5 × 5 in.	6 × 17 cm	
240 mm	5 × 7 in.	5 × 5 in.	
300 mm	8 × 10 in.	9 × 9 in.	

[a]Specific lens manufacturer's recommendations may vary.
[b]Other formats may be accommodated with magnification restrictions.

Table 7.3 Subtractive and additive systems for colour printing

Filters	Transmit	Absorb
	Subtractive (Cyan, Magenta, Yellow filters)	
Cyan	Green & Blue Light	Red Light
Magenta	Red & Blue Light	Green Light
Yellow	Red & Green Light	Blue Light
	Additive (Red, Green, Blue filters)	
Red	Red Light	Green & Blue Light
Green	Green Light	Red & Blue Light
Blue	Blue Light	Red & Green Light

Table 7.4 Colour Correction Table for Printing Colour Negatives

If overall colour balance is:	Action with additive filters	Action with subtractive filters
Too Red	Increase red filter exposure	Increase magenta and yellow filtration or decrease cyan filtration
Too Green	Increase green filter exposure	Decrease magenta filtration
Too Blue	Increase blue filter exposure	Decrease yellow filtration
Too Cyan	Decrease red filter exposure	Decrease yellow and magenta filtration or increase cyan filtration
Too Magenta	Decrease green filter exposure	Increase magenta filtration
Too Yellow	Decrease blue filter exposure	Increase yellow filtration

Table 7.5 Colour Correction Table for Printing Slides or Transparencies

If overall colour balance is:	Action with additive filters	Action with subtractive filters
Too Red	Decrease red filter exposure	Increase cyan filtration or decrease yellow and magenta filtration
Too Green	Decrease green filter exposure	Increase magenta filtration or subtract cyan and yellow filtration
Too Blue	Decrease blue filter exposure	Increase yellow filtration or subtract magenta and cyan filtration
Too Cyan	Increase red filter exposure	Decrease cyan filtration or increase magenta and yellow filtration
Too Magenta	Increase green filter exposure	Decrease magenta filtration or add yellow and cyan filtration
Too Yellow	Increase blue filter exposure	Decrease yellow filtration or add magenta and cyan filtration

Table 7.6 Trouble Shooting when printing colour negatives

Common Problems	Reason and Action
White spots or specks	Dust. Clean the negative to remove the dust.
Streaks, nonuniformity	Improper agitation during processing.
Print contrast too flat	Developer is exhausted or excessively diluted, the paper has been fogged. Check safelights.
High contrast with cyan stain	The developer is too concentrated.
Colour stains in highlights	Contaminated developer, developer too warm, exhausted stop bath, or developer out of date.
Blue-green or reddish spots	Exhausted stop bath.
Bluish black tones	Developer too dilute or developing time too short.
Prints too dark	Exposure time too long, developer too warm or too concentrated.
Prints too light	Exposure time too short or developer too cold or too dilute.
Low colour saturation	Insufficient exposure time, or developer too cold or exhausted.
Pink streaks	Water condensation on the paper before processing.
White areas on print	Fixer contaminated when handling paper before developing.

Table 7.7 Properties of the Major Developing Agents

Common Name	Hydroquinone	Chloro-hydro quinone	Catechol	Pyrogallol	para-Aminophenol	Amidol
Scientific names	1,4-Dihydroxy-benzene; para-dihydroxy-benzene	2-Chloro- 1,4-di-hydroxyben-zene 2-chloro-1,4 benzenediol	1,2-Dihydroxy-benzene; ortho-dihydroxy-benzene	Pyrogallic acid; 1,2,3-trihy-droxy-benzene; 1,2,3-benzene triol	4-Amino-1-hydroxy-benzene hydro-chloride; para-hydroxyaniline	2,4-Diaminophenol dihydrochloride
Commercial names	Quinol Tecquinol, Hydroquinol	Adurol, Chloroquinol	Pyrocatechin	Piral, Pyro	Activol, Azol Kodelon, Para, Rhodinal	Acorl Dianol
Form	Needle-shaped crystals	Needles or leaflets	Needles from water	White crystals	Free base: plates from water. Hydrochloride salt: crystalline	Crystals
Molecular weight	110.11	144.56	110.11	126.11	Free base: 109.12 Hydrocholoride salt: 145.5	197.01

Table 7.7 continued

Common Name	Hydroquinone	Chloro-hydro quinone	Catechol	Pyrogallol	para-Aminophenol	Amidol
Melting point (°C)	170	103	105	131.133	Free base: 190. Hydrochloride salt: decomposes about 306	205
Solubility in water (g in 100 ml at 20°C)	8	92	30	40	Free base: 1.2. Hydrochloride salt: 10.	25
Solubility in solvents	Soluble in alcohol and ether. Slightly soluble in benzene.	Soluble in alcohol. Slightly soluble in ether and chloroform.	Soluble in alcohol, benzene, chloroform, ether, pyridine.	Soluble in alcohol and ether. Slightly soluble in benzene and chloroform.	Free base soluble in alcohol and ethyl methyl ketone, slightly soluble in ether, almost insoluble in benzene and chloroform.	Free base is slightly soluble in alcohol and acetone, very slightly soluble in ether and chloroform.

Table 7.7 continued

Common Name	Hydroquinone	Chloro-hydro quinone	Catechol	Pyrogallol	para-Aminophenol	Amidol
					Hydrochloride salt is soluble in alcohol and slightly soluble in ether.	Hydrochloride salt is soluble in alcohol.
Human toxicity	Relatively safe in very low concentrations. Ingestion of 1 g or more may cause serious complications. Contact with skin may cause dermatitis.		Can cause eczematous dermatitis. Ingestion can cause very serious complications. Avoid contact with large areas of skin.	Severe poisoning may result from percutaneous absorption. Inhalation can cause asthma.	Can cause dermatitis and skin sensitization. Inhalation can cause asthma.	Pure compound or oxidation products may cause eczematoid contact dermatitis or bronchial asthma.

Table 7.7 continued

Common Name	Metol	Glycin	diamine	L-Ascorbic Acid	Phenidone
Scientific names	Monomethyl-para-aminophenol sulphate; para-methyl-amino-phenol sulphate	para-(Hydroxyphenyl) glycine; para-hydroxy-phenyl-amino acetic acid	para-Diamino-benzene; 1,4-diaminobenzene	L-Xyloascorbic acid; hexuronic acid	1-Phenyl-3-pyrazolidone: 1-phenyl-3-pyrazlidi-none
Commercial names	Elon, Genol, Graphol, Pictol, Photol, Rhodol	Athenon, Glycin, Monazol, Iconyl	Free base: Diamine, Paramine, Metacarbol, Hydrochloride salt: Diamine H, P.D.H., p.p.d.	Vitamin C, many pharmaceutical names such as Ascorin, Cevitex, Cevimin	Phenidone, Graphidone
Form	Crystal	Leaflets from water	White crystals	Crystals (plates or needles)	Leaflets or needles from benzene
Molecular weight	344.38	167.16	108.14	176.12	162.19
Melting point (°C)	Free base: 87 Sulphate salt: 260 with	Browns at 200, begins to melt at 220, completely	Freebase: 145–147. Hydrochloride salt: Decomposes	190–192 some decomposition	121

Table 7.7 continued

Common Name	Metol	Glycin	diamine	L-Ascorbic Acid	Phenidone
	decomposition	melted at 247 with decomposition	without melting.		
Solubility in water (g in 100 ml at 20°C)	4	0.02	1	30	2
Solubility in solvents	Freebase very soluble in alcohol, ether, and hot water. Sulphate salt slightly soluble in alcohol and ether, insoluble in benzene.	Low solubility in alcohol, acetone, ether, and benzene.	Freebase solution in alcohol, chloroform, ether Hydrochloride salt soluble slightly in alcohol and ether.	Soluble in alcohol and propylene glycol. Insoluble in ether, chlorofom, benzene.	Soluble in alcohol and benzene. Almost insoluble in ether.
Human toxicity	Can cause skin irrtation or sensitization		Pure compound or oxidation products may cause eczematoid contact dermatitis or bronchial asthma.	Essential vitamin in human nutrition.	Low oral toxicity. No reported cases of dermatitis.

Table 7.8 Phenidone-Hydroquinone Fine-Grain Developer

	ID-68	ID-68R
Warm water (125°F [50°C])	750 ml	750 ml
Sodium sulphite (anhydrous of desiccated)	85 g	85 g
Hydroquinone	5 g	8 g
Borax	7 g	7 g
Boric acid	2 g	–
Phenidone	0.13 g	0.22 g
Potassium bromide	1 g	–
Cold water to make	1 litre	1 litre
Dilution	0	Add to ID-68 to maintain level
Time	8 to 10 min, 20°C (68°F)	

Table 7.9 Contrast developers

Ingredient[a]	Kodak D-19	Kodak D-72	Kodak D-8	Ilford ID-13	Ilford ID-72	Wiedermann Document	Wiedermann PQ X-Ray	Willcock No. 2
Water (125°F[52°C])	500 ml	500 ml	750 ml	750 ml	750 ml	750 ml	750 ml	750 ml
Metol	2.0	3.0	–	–	–	–	–	–
Sodium sulphite desicated	90.0	45.0	90.9	–	72.0	120	150	100
Potassium metabisulphite	–	–	–	12.5	–	–	–	–
Hydroquinone	8.0	12.0	45.0	12.5	8.8	26	20	30
Phenidone	–	–	–	–	0.22	1.0	1.0	1.5
Sodium carbonate, monohydrate	52.5	80.0	–	–	48.0	–	–	–
Potassium carbonate	–	–	–	–	–	110	75	–
Sodium hydroxide	–	–	37.5	–	–	–	–	25
Potassium hydroxide	–	–	–	25	–	–	–	–
Potassium bromide	5.0	2.0	30.0	12.5	4.0	15.0	8.0	3.5
Benzotriazole	–	–	–	–	0.1	1.0	0.5	1.0
Cold water to make	1.0 litre	1.0 litre	1.0 litre	1.0 litre	1.0 litre	1.0 litre	1.0 litre	1.0 litre
Dilution	None	None	2:1	None	None	1:2	1:2	None
Time (min at 20°C)	5	1 to 3	2	3 to 5	5	2 to 4	5	1/2 to 1

[a]All quantities are in grams unless indicated otherwise.

7.10 Fixers

Simple Acid Fixer

Sodium thiosulphate	8–10	ounces	200–300	grams
Sodium bisulphite or potassium metabisulphite	1	ounce	25	grams
Water to make	40	fluid ounces	1	litre

Chrome Alum Fixer

Chrome alum	12.5	grams
Sodium metabisulphite	12.5	grams
Sodium sulphite, anhydrous	6.25	grams
Sodium thiosulphate (5 H_2O)	400	grams
Water to make	1	litre

Potassium Alum fixer

Sodium thiosulphate (5 H_20)	240	grams
Sodium sulphite, anhydrous	15	grams
Boric acid	7.5	grams
Acetic acid, 28%	48	ml
Potassium alum	15	grams
Water to make	1	litre

Rapid Fixer

Ammonium thiosulphate	135	grams
Boric acid	7	grams
Sodium acetate, anhydrous	10	grams
Sodium metabilsulphite	5	grams
Sodium sulphite, anhydrous	6	grams
Water to make	1	litre

7.11 Fixing times and capacities

Sodium Thiosulphate Fixers

Films	7–10	minutes
Fibre-base papers	3–5	minutes
RC papers	2	minutes maximum

Ammonium Thiosulphate Fixers

Films	2–5	minutes
Fibre-base papers	1/2–5	minutes
RC papers	2	minutes maximum

Film Material	Number per Litre of 25% Sodium Thiosulphate Solution
135–20 film	60
135–36 film	30
120 film	30
4 × 5 inch film	100
8 × 10 inch film	30

Table 7.12 Fixing times with hypo-clearing bath

	Without Hypo-Clearing	With Hypo-Clearing
Films	20–30 min	5 in
RC-paper	4 min	Not rec.
Single-weight fibre-based paper	60 min	10 min
Double-weight fibre-based paper	120 min	20 min

Table 7.13 Hydrogen ion concentration/pH

The pH and pOH Scales

Hygrogen ions (moles per litre)			pH Scale			pOH Scale		Hydroxyl Ions (moles per litre)
1.0	or	10^{-0}	0	Highly acid	14	10^{-14}	or	0.00000000000001
0.1		10^{-1}	1	↑	13	10^{-13}		0.0000000000001
0.01		10^{-2}	2		12	10^{-12}		0.000000000001
0.001		10^{-3}	3		11	10^{-11}		0.00000000001
0.0001		10^{-4}	4		10	10^{-10}		0.0000000001
0.00001		10^{-5}	5		9	10^{-9}		0.000000001
0.000001		10^{-6}	6		8	10^{-8}		0.00000001
0.0000001		10^{-7}	7	Neutral	7	10^{-7}		0.0000001
0.00000001		10^{-8}	8		6	10^{-6}		0.000001
0.000000001		10^{-9}	9		5	10^{-5}		0.00001
0.0000000001		10^{-10}	10		4	10^{-4}		0.0001
0.00000000001		10^{-11}	11		3	10^{-3}		0.001
0.000000000001		10^{-12}	12	↓	2	10^{-2}		0.01
0.0000000000001		10^{-13}	13		1	10^{-1}		0.0
0.00000000000001		10^{-14}	14	Highly alkaline	0	10^{-0}		1.0

Table 7.14 ISO Standard for Viewing Prints and Transparencies

	Surround Reflection Density	Colour-Rendering Index	Luminance (cd/m^2)	Illuminance (lux)	Illumination Uniformity Edge/Centre	Spectral Power Distribution
Transparencies						
Large	>1.0	90	1300 ± 300	–	0.75	D_{50}
Small	Opaque	90	1300 ± 300	–	0.40	D_{50}
Prints						
Critical appraisal	>0.50	90	–	Inspection 20000 ± 500 Practical 500 ± 125	0.75	D_{50}
Routine inspection	>0.20	85	–	800 ± 200	0.60	D_{30}–D_{50}
Judging and exhibiting	>0.20	85	–	800 ± 200	0.60	D_{30}–D_{50}

Field of Application. The standard describes:
1. Conditions for viewing large and small transparencies for critical appraisal or for comparison with other objects or images
2. Conditions for viewing reflection photographic and photomechanical prints for critical appraisal or for comparison with other objects or images
3. Conditions for viewing reflection prints to aid in routine inspection
4. Conditions for judging or exhibiting reflection prints

*ANSI PH 2.30 – *1985 Viewing Conditions – Photographic Prints, Transparencies, and Photomechanical Reproductions.*

(A *Catalogue* of ANSI *Standards* and the *Standards* themselves can be obtained from the American National Standards Institute, 1430 Broadway, New York, NY 10018.)

8 Film and video data

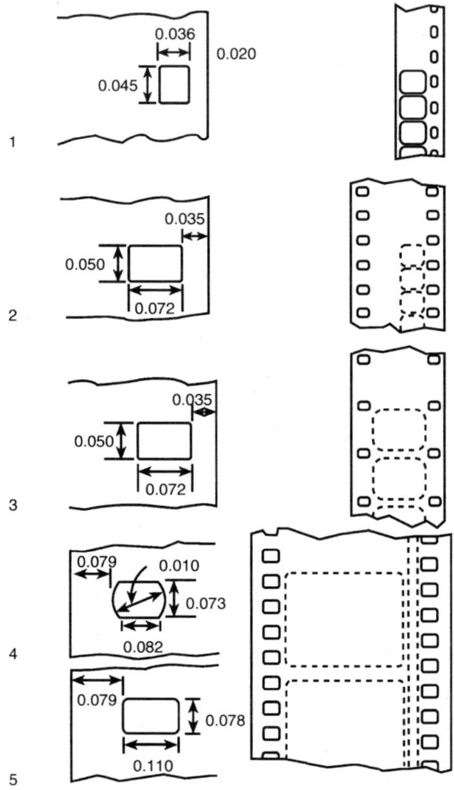

Figure 8.1 Perforation types and sizes. (1) Super-8-mm; (2) standard double-8-mm film; (3) standard 16-mm film; (4) negative perforation of standard 35-mm film; (5) positive perforation of standard 35-mm film. All dimensions are in inches.

8.2 Glossary of selected video terms

A & B roll editing A procedure where two or more videotapes are fed into an editor and mixed onto the edit tape.
Address The location of a segment of tape on a reel given by its frame counter in and out points.
Arc To move a camera on a dolly in a left- or right- direction while keeping the same distance from centre stage (as though it were tethered to that point).
Assemble edit The transfer of video, audio, and control track signals from a source tape to an edit tape during editing.
BNC A video cable connector with a locking collar.
Boom A microphone stand with a long horizontal arm is counter-balanced; used to position a microphone above the set.
Camcorder A video camera and videotape recorder combined into one piece of equipment.
Cathode ray tube (CRT) The large picture tube receiver or monitor.
Character generator A kind of electronic typewriter that is used to add text to videotapes.
Coax[ial] A type of video cable with a thin single strand wire inside a plastic tube that is wrapped with a woven wire and covered with insulation; like the antenna cable television.
Composite signal A combined video and audio signal.
Control track An electronic signal on a videotape that videos a timing reference for the electronic sensing of the visual and audio imagery; like sprocket holes in motion picture film.
CU (closeup) A video shot that, for a person, covers the area of a head-and-shoulders portrait.
Cut To switch instantly from one shot to another with a switcher or effects generator.
Dolly To move a camera toward (*dolly in*) or away from (*dolly out*) centre stage. A tripod platform with wheels.
Dropout A place on a videotape where the magnetic coating is worn or damaged; this causes a white fleck in the picture.
Dropout compensator An electronic device in a receiver or VCR that replaces dropout flecks with the last bit of the imagery scanned in order to give the visual effect of continuity in the quality of the picture.
Dub To add sound to video after recording the visual imagery. To copy video or audio tapes.
Editing log A list of the shots on a videotape recorded by their address on the frame counter.
Effects generator A device used in editing that permits the use of special effects (different kinds of fades and wipes) when making a transition from one shot to another. Can also be used as an audio mixer. Similar to a switcher but does not have a synchronization generator.
Electronic News Gathering (ENG) The use of a camera outside of the studio and in a portable configuration.
Establishing Shot A long shot.
Extreme Closeup (XCU) Very tightly framed image—usually less than 3 feet—used to show small detail.

Fade; dissolve To move slowly from one shot to another with a switcher or effects generator.
Field One-half of the scan of a picture. See also: *Frame*.
Focus To adjust the lens for image sharpness.
Format The size of videotape. Also used to indicate a type of program.
Frame Two scans (fields) of a picture making one complete image (frame). Scan rate is 50 fields, 20 frames, per second.
Insert To add a portion of one shot into (usually an upper corner of) another; adds background interest or information.
Insert edit The transfer of either video or audio signals, or both from a source VCR to an edit VCR without the transfer of the control track.
Key; chroma key An editing or switching effect that cuts one image into another; used to add titles and graphics. Chroma key uses colour (normally blue) to drop background from the shot to be keyed in.
Lavaliere A small microphone that is worn attached to the lapel.
Long shot (LS) A wide-angle picture that includes more background that it does figure; used to establish context.
Medium shot (MS) About the equivalent of a three-quarter pose in portraiture.
Medium Long Shot (MLS) Similar to a full-length portrait or small group shot.
Microphone Mixer/Audio Mixer; Mic Mixer A device that accepts multiple audio inputs, has volume controls for each, and feeds one signal to record.
Pan To move the camera lens to the left or right in a horizontal motion.
Pedestal To raise (*pedestal up*) or lower (*pedestal down*) the camera, or to move it around. A large, studio-type camera stand with wheels that is operated hydraulically or electronically.
Pixillation An effect used to make inanimate objects appear to move around; achieved by repeatedly running a short segments of tape and moving the object around in the shot. When played back, the object *moves* as though under its own power.
Pot[entiometer] A volume or gain knob (coil) on a microphone mixer, switcher, or lighting control board.
Preroll The distance a VCR rewinds a tape before an edit in order to synchronize it with the other VCR; usually 5 seconds.
Radio Frequency (RF) A means of video distribution via a coaxial cable with multiple composite (video and audio) signals; requires a receiver.
Safety Shot In multiple camera operations, one camera is kept on a complete view of the scene that can be used if one or more of the other cameras fail during taping.
Skew An adjustment of the VCR's tape tension; used to stabilize the upper portion of a picture.
Source VTR(s) The VCR(s) used to feed video signals into the edit VTR.
Super[impose] To layer one shot atop another by means of a switcher.
Switcher A device that accepts multiple video inputs, syn-

chronizes the scan cycles of the cameras, has an intercom for studio crew communication, and offers multiple special effects in the process of cutting or fading to the signal that is sent to record.

Synch[ronization] The aligning of the travel of equal scan guns on two or more camera so the pictures are timed together and can be mixed by a switcher without rolling.

Tilt To move the camera lens up or down.

Time Base Corrector (TBC) A postproduction device used to filter and strengthen (clean up) the control track signals on tapes made with different pieces of equipment.

Tracking An adjustment of the VCR used to stabilize a picture.

Video Toaster A microprocessor that generates computer graphics and special effects for video applications.

Truck To move the camera to the left or right parallel to the front of the stage.

VCR/VTR Video cassette/tape recorder.

Videographer An image maker that uses video.

White Balance (WB) To set the video camera for the colour temperature of the lighting being used; similar to selecting daylight (5500 K) or tungsten (3200 K) film for still photography.

Wild Sound Audio that is recorded independently of the video.

XCU (extreme closeup) Very tight framing; full-face of a person or details on small object.

Zoom A type of lens with variable focal lengths. To adjust the focal length from wide-angle to telephoto (zoom in) or from telephoto to wide-angle (zoom out).

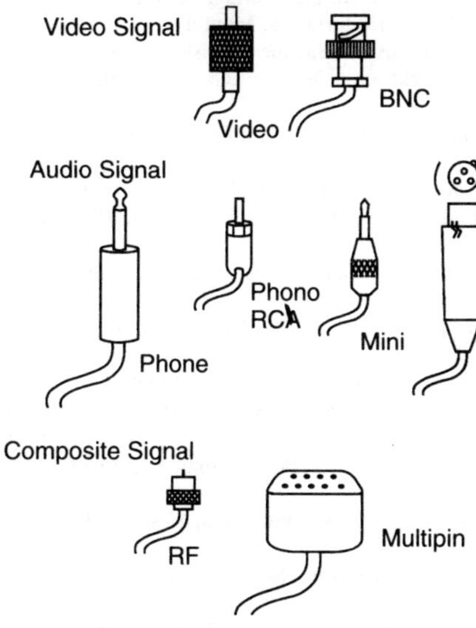

Figure 8.3 Cables. Cable connectors.

9 Photographic periodicals and publications

Current Periodicals Photography periodical publishing is a volatile area, marked by an endless series of introductions and inevitable cessations. The following list is drawn from the hundreds of titles in print at the time of compilation. It represents major categories of photography serials and includes examples from throughout the world, although it favours titles published in the United States and Western Europe. More complete listings are available in Ulrich's International Periodicals Dictionary (3 vols. New Providence, N.J.: R.R. Bowker, Biennial) and The Standard Periodical Directory (New York: Oxbridge Communications, Inc. Annual).

General Coverage

American Photo. New York: Diamandis Communications. Bimonthly.

Asahi Camera. Tokyo: Asahi Shimbun. Monthly.

British Journal of Photography. London: Henry Greenwood and Co. Weekly.

Focus. Amsterdam: Focus. Quarterly.

Fotografia. Bucharest: Associatia Artistilor Fotografi din Romania. Quarterly.

Fotografisk Tidskrift. Stockholm: Göstaflemming. Bimonthly.

Fotomagazin. Munich: Ringier Verlag. Monthly.

IrisFoto. São Paulo: Editoria Iris. Monthly.

Photo. Paris: Editions des Savanes. 10 issues/year.

Photo Life. Markham, Ontario: Camar Publications. 10 issues/year.

*Der Photograp*h. Vienna: Verlag für Photographische Literatur. Monthly.

PhotoMagazine. Paris: Editions Paul Montel. Monthly.

Photo Reporter. Paris: Société Photovision, 1907 to date, monthly.

Photographers Forum. Santa Barbara: Serbin Communications. Quarterly.

Photographic Journal. Bath: The Royal Photographic Society. Monthly.

Photographie. Schaffhausen: Novapress. Monthly.

Photography. London: Argus Specialist Publications. Monthly.

Progresso Fotografico. Milan: Editrice Progresso. Monthly.

PSA Journal. Oklahoma City: Photographic Society of America. Monthly.

Valokuva. Helsinki: Suomen Valokuvajärjestöjen Keskusliitto Finnfoto. Monthly.

Sovetskoye Foto. Moscow: Soyuz Zhurnalistov U.S.S.R. Monthly.

View Camera. Sacramento: Steve Simmons Photography. Bimonthly.

Zoom. Paris: Editions Zoom. Bi-monthly.

Fine-Art Photography, Photographic History, and Criticism

AFT: Rivista di Storia e Fotografia. Prato: Archivo Fotografico Toscano. Semi-annual.

Afterimage. Rochester, N.Y.: Visual Studies Workshop. 10 issues/year.

Aperture. New York: Aperture Foundation. Quarterly.

Les Cahiers de la Photographie. Paris: L'Association de Critique Contemporaine en Photographie. 3 issues/year.

Camera Austria. Graz: Camera Austria. Quarterly.

Camera Canada. Scarborough, Ontario: National Association for Photographic Art. Quarterly.

Camera International. Paris: Camera International. Quarterly.

Cliches. Bruxelles: Editions du Stratege. Monthly.

Creative Camera. London: CC Publishing. Bi-monthly.

Déjà-vu. Tokyo: Photo-Planète Co. Quarterly.

Edice RF. Prague: Orbis. Quarterly.

European Photography. Göttingen: Andreas Müller-Pohle. Quarterly.

Foto. Leusden: Foto. 10 issues/year

Fotogeschichte. Marburg: Jonas Verlag für Kunst und Literatur. Quarterly.

Fotologia. Florence: Fratelli Alinari Editrice. Irregular.

History of Photography. London: Taylor and Francis. Quarterly.

Madame De Vue. Amsterdam: Madame De Vue. Quarterly.

October. Cambridge, Mass.: MIT Press. Quarterly.

Perspektief. Rotterdam: Perspektief Centrum voor Fotografie. Quarterly.

Photo Review. Langhorne, Pa.: The Photo Review. Quarterly.

Photographic Collector. New York: Consultant Press. Monthly.

Photographica. New York: American Photographic Historical Society. Quarterly.

Photographies Magazine. Paris PME SARL. 10 issues/year.

Photoresearcher. Croydon, Surrey, England: European Society for the History of Photography. Semi-annual.

Photovision. Madrid PhotoVision. Quarterly.

Pinhole Journal. San Lorenzo, N.M.: Pinhole Resource. 3 issues/year.

Portfolio Magazine. Edinburgh: Photography Workshop. Quarterly.

La Recherche Photographique. Paris: Paris Audiovisuel, Maison Europeenne de la Photographie. Université Paris. Semi-annual.

Revista de la Historia de la Fotografia Española. Seville: Sociedad de Historia de la Fotografia Español. Semiannual.

SF Camera-work Quarterly. San Francisco: San Francisco Camerawork. Quarterly.

Stereo World. Columbis, Ohio: National Stereoscopic Association. Bi-monthly.

Ten.8. Birmingham, England: Ten.8 Ltd. Quarterly.

Museum, Gallery, and Art Centre Publications

Archive. Tucson: Center for Creative Photography. Semiannual.

Blackflash. Saskatoon, Saskatchewan: The Photography Gallery. Quarterly.

Center Quarterly. Woodstock, N.Y: Center for Photography at Woodstock. Quarterly.

C.E.PA. Quarterly. Buffalo, N.Y: Center for Exploratory and Perceptual Art. Quarterly.

Contact Sheet. Syracuse, N.Y: Light Work. 5 issues/year.

Frame-work. Los Angeles: Los Angeles Center for Photographic Studies. 3 issues/year.

Image. Rochester, N.Y.: International Museum of Photography at George Eastman House. Quarterly.

Katalog. Odense, Denmark: Museet for Fotokunst. Quarterly.

MOPA. San Diego: Museum of Photographic Arts. Quarterly.

Nueva Luz. New York: En Foco. Quarterly.

Photo Paper. Pittsburgh: Blatent Image/Silver Eye. Quarterly.

Photofile. Paddington, NSW: Australian Centre for Photography. Quarterly.

Photographie Ouverte. Brussels: Echevinat de la Culture de la Ville de Charleroi et de la Communaute Francaise de Belgique. Bi-monthly.

Spot. Houston: Houston Center for photography. 3 issues/year

Untitled. San Francisco: Friends of Photography. Irregular.

Views. Boston: Photographic Resource Center at Boston University. 3 issues/year.

Applied Photography

Applied Arts Quarterly. Dons Mills, Ontario: Applied Arts. Quarterly.

Art Direction. New York: Advertising Trade Publications. Monthly.

Communication Arts. Palo Alto, Calif.: Coyne and Blanchard. 8 issues/year.

Graphics. Zurich: Graphis Press. Bi-monthly.

Industrial Photography. Melville, N.Y.: PTN Publishing. Monthly.

Journal of Biological Photography. Chapel Hill, N.C.: Biological Photographic Association. Quarterly.

Journal of Audio-Visual Media in Medicine. London: Butterworth-Heinemann for the Institute of Medical Illustrators. Quarterly.

Lürzer's Int'l Archive. New York: American Showcase. Bimonthly.

News Photographer. Durham, N.C.: National Press Photographers Association. Monthly.

Photo/Design. New York: BPI Communications. Bimonthly

Select. Düsseldorf: Moser and Colby. 3 issues/year.

Career and Professional Information

ASMP Bulletin. New York: American Society of Magazine Photographers. Monthly.

Entry: A Guide to Photographic Competitors and Juried Exhibitions. Ann Arbor, Mich.: Entry. 10 issues/year.

Guilfoyle Report. New York: AG Editions. Quarterly.
Kodak Studio Light. Rochester, N.Y.: Eastman Kodak. Semiannual .
Photo District News. New York: Photo District News. Monthly.
Photoletter. Osceola, Wis.: PhotoSource International. Monthly.
Picture Professional. New York: American Society of Picture Professionals. Quarterly.
Professional Photographe. Paris: Profession Photographe. Bimonthly.
Professional Photographer. Essex, England: Market Link Publishing, Monthly.
Professional Photographer. Des Plaines, Ill.: Professional Photographers of America Publications and Events. Monthly.
Rangefinder. Santa Monica, Calif.: The Rangefinder Publishing Co. Monthly.
Studio Photography. Melville, N.Y.: PTN Publishing. Monthly
.

Education

Exposure. Boulder, Colo.: Society for Photographic Education. Quarterly.
Ilford Photo Instructor Newsletter. Paramus, N.J.: Ilford Photo. Irregular.
Photo Educator. Rochester, N.Y: Eastman Kodak. Irregular.
Photoeducation. Cambridge, Mass.: Polaroid Corporation. Quarterly.

Photographic Industry

International Contact. Ratingen: C.A.T. Verlag Blömer. 6 issues/year.
Japan Camera Trade News: JCTN. Tokyo: Genyosha Publication.. Monthly.
Mini Lab Focus. Jackson, Mich.: Photo Marketing Association International. Monthly.
Photo Business. New York: Billboard Publications. Monthly.
Photo Lab Management. Santa Monica, Calif.: PLM Publishing. Monthly.
Photo Made in Italy. Milan: Mediaspazio. Quarterly.
Photo Marketing. Jackson, Mich.: Photo Marketing Association International. Monthly.
Photo Marketing Newsline. Jackson, Mich.: Photo Marketing Association International. Semi-monthly.
Photographic Processing. Melville, N.Y.: PTN Publishing. Monthly.
PhotoVideo. Toronto: AVS Publishing. 9 issues/year.

Photographic science

Image Technology: *Journal of the BKSTS*. London: British Kinematograph, Sound, and Television Society. Monthly.
Journal of Imaging Science and Technology. Springfield, Va.: The Society for Imaging Science and Technology. Bimonthly.
Journal of Information Recording Materials. Berlin: Akademie Verlag. Bi-monthly.
Journal of Photographic Science. Bath: Royal Photographic Society of Great Britain. Bi-monthly.

Photographic Science and Photochemistry. Beijing: Science Press. Quarterly.
Scientific and Applied Photography and Cinematography (cover-to-cover English translation of Zhurnal Nauchnoi i Prikladnoi Fotografii i Kinematografii). New York: Gordon and Breach. Bi-monthly.
SMPTE Journal. White Plains, N.Y.: Society of Motion Picture and Television Engineers. Monthly.

Photographic Methods and Techniques

Camera and Darkroom Photography. Beverly Hills, Calif.: L.F.P Monthly.
Camera Art. Tokyo: CamerArt. Monthly.
Darkroom and Creative Camera Technique. Niles, Ill.: Preston Publications. Bi-monthly.
Outdoor Photographer. Los Angeles: Werner Publishing. Monthly.
Petersen's Photographic. Los Angeles: Petersen Publishing. Monthly.
Photo Answers. Peterborough, England: EMAP Pub. Monthly.
Photo Pro. Tittusville Fla.: PhotoPro of Titusville. Bimonthly.
Photo Technique International. English ed. Munich: Verlag Photo Technik International. Quarterly; German ed. Munich: Verlag Photo Technik International. Bi-monthly.
Photomethods. Des Plaines, Ill.: PPA Publications and Events. Monthly.
Popular Photography. New York: Hachette Magazines. Monthly.
Shutterbug. Titusville, Fla.: Patch Publishing. Monthly.

Manufacturers' Periodicals

Hasselblad Forum. English, German, and Swedish editions. Göteborg: Victor Hasselblad Aktiebolag. Quarterly.
International Photography. Rochester, N.Y.: Eastman Kodak. Semi-annual.
Kodak Studio Light. Rochester, N.Y.: Eastman Kodak. Semiannual.
Kodak Tech Bits. Rochester, N.Y.: Eastman Kodak Co. Irregular.
Leica Fotografie International. English, French, and German editions. Frankfurt am Main: Umschau Verlag. 8 issues/year.
Nikon Salon. Tokyo: Nikon Optical Company. Quarterly.
Pentax Life. Englewood, Colo.: Pentax Corporation. 3 issues/year.

Annuals and Yearbooks

American Photography. New York: American Photography.
Advertising Photography in Japan. Tokyo: Kodansha.
Communication Arts Photography Annual (August issue of *Communication Arts*). Palo Alto, Calif.: Coyne and Blanchard.
Graphis Photo. Zurich: Graphics Press.
Photography Yearbook. Surbiton, Surrey, England: Fountain Press.

10 Miscellaneous

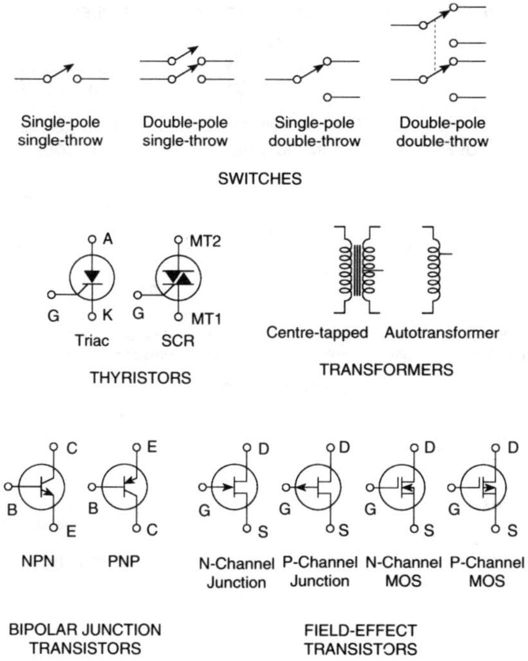

Figure 10.1 Electronics. Graphic symbols commonly used in electronic circuit diagrams.

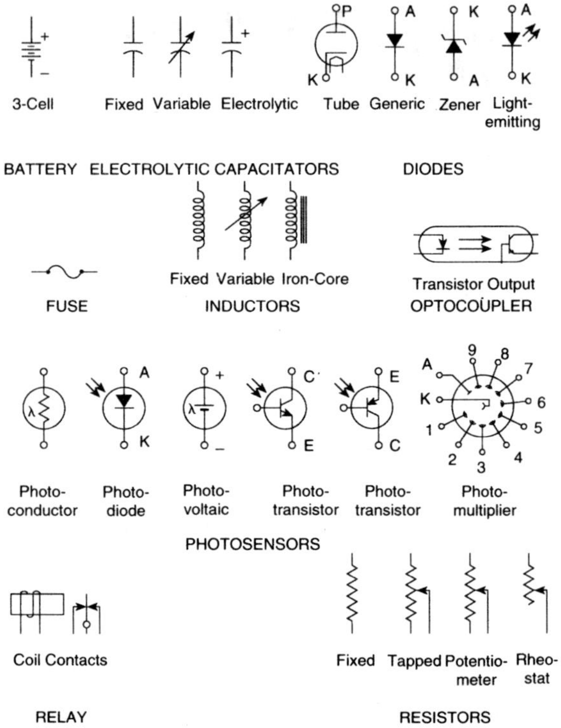

3-Cell
BATTERY
Fixed
Variable
Electrolytic
ELECTROLYTIC CAPACITATORS
P
K
Tube
A
K
Generic
K
A
Zener
A
K
Light-emitting
DIODES
FUSE
Fixed
Variable
Iron-Core
INDUCTORS
Transistor Output
OPTOCOUPLER
Photo-conductor
A
K
Photo-diode
+
–
Photo-voltaic
C
E
Photo-transistor
E
C
Photo-transistor
A
K
1
2
3
4
5
6
7
8
9
Photo-multiplier
PHOTOSENSORS
Coil Contacts
RELAY
Fixed
Tapped
Potentio-meter
Rheo-stat
RESISTORS

Table 10.2 Imaging Technologies, Systems, and Applications

Technologies	Systems	Applications
1. Silver halide photography	A. Monochrome (black and white)	• Black-and-white negatives, prints, transparencies • Instant black-and-white prints, negatives, slides • Instant additive colour slides • Dry silver–hard copy, overheads
	B. Colour chromogenic systems	• Photofinished colour prints, slides, transparencies • Colour output from electronic imagery
	C. Colour nonchromogenic systems	• Instant colour prints, transparencies • Dye bleach colour prints, transparencies
2. Nonsilver chemical photography	A. Photopolymer and resist systems	• Plates, proofs, resists–circuit boards and chips
	B. Diazo and vesicular systems	• Plates, proofs, resists–circuit boards and chips, overheads, microfilms
	C. Dye imaging – photochromics, leucodye systems	• Proofs, duplications
	D. Thermal systems	• Nonimpact printing, overheads
3. Graphic arts and mechanical imaging	A. Press printing systems • Lithography • Gravure • Letterpress – flexography • Screens	• Press printing • Circuit board printing

Table 10.2 continued

Technologies	Systems	Applications
	B. Automated typing systems	• Impact printing
	C. Ink-jet systems	• Nonimpact printing
4. Electrophotographic imaging	A. Xerographic systems	• Plain paper offset
	B. Electrofaxic systems	• Office copy, proofing systems, litho plates for G/A, slide copiers
	C. Laser scanning xerography	• Nonimpact printing
	D. Electrostatic, dielectric, and magnetostatic systems	• Nonimpact printing
5. Electronic imaging	A. Television	• Television, home video • Taped playbacks–broadcast and VCR
	B. Electronic taking imagery	• Graphic arts prepress systems • Medical CRT applications • Remote sensing, infrared, radar • Airport x-radiograph devices
	C. Computer generated imagery	• Word processors, phototypesetters • CAD/CAM • Facsimile • Computer output microfilm

Source: Alan Shepp, "Introduction to Images and Imaging," John Sturge et al. *Image Processing and Materials,* New York: Van Nostrand Reinhold, 1989, p.3. Courtesy Van Nostrand Reinhold.

Table 10.3 Comparison of Imaging Modalities

Imaging System	Amplification Factor	Exposure Energy (μJ–cm^{-2})	Resolving Power (l-mm^{-1})	Unsensitized Sensitivity Range (nm)	Sensitized Sensitivity Range (nm)
Silver halide–fast	10^9	5×10^{-4}	50	<200–500	Up to 1300
Silver halide–medium	0.2×10^9	10^{-2}	150	<200–500	Up to 1300
Dry silver (3M)	10^6	10^{-1}–20	100–400	<200–500	
Vidicon tube	10^{10}	10^{-5}	5	<400–800	
Charge-coupled device		10^{-3}	600	400–1000	Up to 9 μm
Electrophotography	10^6–10^7	10^{-1}	20–>1000	280–400	Up to 830
Photopolymerization	$>10^6$	10^2–10^5	500	280–400	Up to 600
Photoresist	$>10^3$	4×10^3–10^5	>1000	<200–500	ion beam, x-ray electron beam
Diazo	1	3×10^4–10^7	>1000	350–450	
Photochromism	1	10^4–10^5	1000	uv-vis, narrow bands	
Thermal transfer dye diffusion trans.	–	–	20	–	–
Ink Jet	–	–	4–12	–	–

Table 10.4 Defective colour vision (colour blindness)

Type of Defect	Colours Confused	Incidence Men	Incidence Women
Protanopia	All reddish and greenish; reds dark	1.0%	0.02%
Deuteranopia	All reddish and greenish	1.1%	0.01%
Tritanopia	All yellowish and bluish	0.002%	0.001%
Protanomaly	Some reddish and greenish; reds dark	1.0%	0.02%
Deuteranomaly	Some reddish and greenish	4.9%	0.38%
Tritanomaly	Some yellow and bluish	?	?
Rod mono-chromacy	All colours	0.002%	0.002%
Cone mono-chromacy	All colours	Very rare	
Totals		8.0%	0.4%

Table 10.5 Visual Resolution and Minimum Visible Detail at Different Magnifications

		High-Contrast Object		Low-Contrast Object		
Viewing Situation	Magnification	Cycles per mm[1]	μm[2]	Cycles per mm[1]	μm[2]	Structure Visible
Naked eye	1	5	100 (0.1 mm)	1	500 (0.5 mm)	None
Projected with 100 mm lens						
At projector	2½	12½	40	2½	200	None
Halfway from screen	5	25	20	5	100	Little or none
One-tenth distance from screen	25	125	4	25	20	Grain clumps
Microscope	250	1250	0.4	250	2	Single grains
Electron microscope	2500	12500	0.04	2500	0.2	Dye droplets

[1]Resolution

[2]Diameter of smallest visible detail

10.6 Cells and batteries

Most modern photographic equipment needs batteries, and photographiers rely increasingly on other devices that also need portable power. Follow these guidelines to obtain the maximum possible use from a battery or cell.

Choose a single cell or a factory-sealed battery (a battery is a row of cells joined in series or parallel) if possible. Two cells stacked in contact in a battery compartment are less reliable than a single cell with a higher voltage, or a pair of cells with their contacts factory-soldered together.

Pick a cell according to the application: no one type is "best". For details see below, under the different types.

Change light-usage cells regularly: ideally, annually on the same date. Replace them with new cells bought from a dealer with a rapid turnover of stock. Don't replace a cell with the stand-by that has been in the camera bag for a year.

Stock up only with those batteries that are changed often, since few have a shelf life longer than a couple of years. For longer life, store cells at between 10° and 25°C (50° and 77°F), and below 65 per cent relative humidity. Dispose of batteries carefully: don't burn them or they will explode.

Mercury cells Mercury cells have a shelf life of approximately 2½ years and they represent an economic choice for equipment that is infrequently used. They may be the only choice for certain types of photographic equipment.

Silver oxide cells Many button cells fall into this category and they are a more costly alternative to mercury cells. However, they have a number of advantage–they provide a slightly higher voltage, better suited to voltage-critical components, such as liquid-crystal displays. Shelf life is comparable with mercury cells. Silver cells have poor low-temperature characteristics, so keep equipment powered by them under warm clothing when temperatures fall below freezing.

Lithium cells There are two types of lithium cell, but most user-exchangeable cells are of the lithium/manganese type. Some photographic equipment can be powered by a single lithium cell instead of a pair of silver or mercury cells, and the single lithium cell may last slightly longer than the pair of silver cells. However, take care because the voltage from a lithium cell tapers off slowly at the end of its life, leading to erratic performance rather than complete failure. The alternatives, by contrast, maintain full power right up to the end.

Zinc-carbon cells The power output of a zinc-carbon cell drops progressively throughout its life–typically, a bulb powered by a zinc-carbon cell will glow yellower as the battery runs down. Consequently, these cells are suitable only for non-critical applications, such as torches.

Magnanese alkaline cells Manganese alkaline cells are

the "bread and butter" of the photographic world, and with good reason. They have a long shelf life (up to 3 years) and provide a high power output. They are also very widely available and perform well even at temperatures as low as –20°C (–4°F).

Rechargeable cells

Nickel cadmium batteries (NiCads) appear at first glance to be the ideal way to cut the cost of battery use, especially if you use apparatus that needs many batteries, such as a motor drive. However, bear these points in mind:

NiCad cells These power cells provide a lower voltage than primary cells of comparable size: 1.25V as opposed to 1.5V. In voltage-critical applications, this may be significant.

Primary cells If weight is a factor, and there are no facilities for recharging, long-life primary cells may be better.

Maintenance

NiCad rechargeables are not "maintenance free", though they may be advertised as such. Regular care and maintenance is needed for maximum capacity.

Charging Even when not in use, a NiCad cell or battery loses power constantly and needs "topping up" periodically. Unfortunately, a meter won't tell you when this is necessary, because NiCad cells maintain their full voltage throughout the duty cycle. Voltage then drops rapidly. Only by monitoring usage will you get a true indication of when you need to recharge.

If you totally drain a NiCad cell, recharge it immediately. Failure to do this may cause irreversible damage to the cell. Never overcharge a NiCad–always observe the manufacturer's recommendations, because overcharging can reduce life. Quick-charge cells are–as the name suggests–specially designed for rapid recharging, and regular NiCads cannot be substituted without the risk of overheating and permanent damage.

Memory effect Few photographers take a fully charged cell and totally drain it. Partial use of a cell's capacity eventually inhibits its ability to deliver full power. To prevent this happening, every three months you should totally exhaust the cells by shorting them through a resistance, such as a torch (flashlamp) bulb until the bulb no longer glows, and then recharge them immediately.

Other battery types

Most other types of cell are specifically engineered for use with a particular piece of equipment. Conventional lead-acid accumulators have now been rendered virtually obsolete by "gell-cells", which have a gelled electrolyte. These are perhaps the ideal bateries for flash applications, since they provide rapid recycling, a marginally increased light output and long life, and many have state-of-charge indicators. They are, however, more expensive than most other types.

Table 10.7 Batteries Comparison of Cells/Batteries

System	Carbon-zinc (Leclanche)	Carbon-zinc (heavy duty)	Alkaline	Silver Oxide	Lithium	Nickel Cadmium
Chemistry						
Anode	Zn	Zn	Zn (powered)	Zn	Li	Cd
Cathode	MnO_2	MnO_2	MnO_2	Ag_2O	MnO_2	$Ni(OH)_3$
Electrolyte	NH_4Cl and $ZnCl_2$	$ZnCl_2$	KOH	KOH or NaOH	$LiSO_2$ with organic solvent	KOH
Rechargeable?	No	No	No	No	No	Yes
Cell voltage	1.5 V	1.5 V	1.5 V	1.5 V	3.0 V	1.25 V
Energy density	Low	Low	Moderate	High	High	High
Shelf life	Fair	Fair	Good	Excellent	Excellent	Good
Cost	Lowest	Low	Moderate	High	High	High
Special characteristics	Lowest cost	Designed for heavier output current	High energy and current capacity	Maintains a constant voltage	10-year shelf life; leakproof	Rechargeable; leakproof

Table 10.7 continued

System	Carbon-zinc (Leclanche)	Carbon-zinc (heavy duty)	Alkaline	Silver Oxide	Lithium	Nickel Cadmium
Best suited for	Intermittent uses such as flashlights	General use performance better than regular zinc-carbon	Continous heavy drain loads such as motor drives	Constant voltage applications; portable light meters, cameras, etc.	Still camera electronics, TV remote controllers, smoke detectors	Power packs for electronic flash, video cameras; portable tools
Limitations	Low energy density; prone to leak	Performance lower than alkaline batteries; prone to leak	More costly than zinc-carbon	Available in a limited number of sizes	Available in limited number of sizes	Does not retain its charge as well as nonchargeable batteries do

Table 10.8 Colour Publishing Systems

Features	Density/Creative	Desktop System	Mid-range System	High-end Prepress
Skill Levels	Low-moderate	Moderate	Moderate-high	High Proprietary
Hardware	Standard	Standard	Blend	Proprietary
Software	Standard	Standard	Blend	Proprietary
Productivity	Low	Low-moderate	Moderate	High
Quality	Low	Low-moderate	Moderate	High
Proofing	B/W laser	Colour thermal	Colour thermal	Traditional/DDCP
Storage Capacity	80 MB+	100 MB +	200 MB +	1 gigabyte+
Output	Proof printer	Imagesetter	Imagesetter	Film recorder
Cost	X	2X	4X	8X

Table 10.9 Motors. Characteristics of Small Motors.

Motor Type	Permanent Magnet (PM)	Coreless Rotor (PM)	Stepper	Synchronous Timer	Shaded Pole	Capacitor Start and Run
Voltage	DC	DC	Pulsed DC	AC	AC	AC
Reversible on start	Yes	Yes	Yes	No	No	Yes
Reversible during run	Yes	Yes	Yes	No	No	Yes
Special characteristics	Energy efficient	Low intertia rotor; fast response	Shaft turns a precise angle for each pulse	Constant speed	Lowest cost	High torque, reversible
Best suited for	Film advance and rewind in cameras	Film advance and rewind in cameras	Metering of film and paper in photofinishing equipment	Timers and clocks	Fans and blowers	Applications requiring frequent cycling
Limitations	Brushes may need replacement	Expensive, brushes may need replacement	Requires expensive electronic controller	Low torque, low speed	Inefficient, low starting torque	

10.10 X-ray precautions

Crossing international frontiers always involves security checks of some description, and usually these include X-rays. The risk involved when film is X-rayed is a hotly debated issue, as is the value of any precautions: the protection offered by lead bags, for example, is not yet proven. There are few statistics available, but one source has estimated that 0.3 per cent of all photographic films processed show some signs of X-ray damage.

Naturally, the best way to make sure that there is no damage to your films is to ask for a hand search of luggage containing film, but this is not always possible. So if you cannot prevent film from being X-rayed, what are the risks?

Photo scientists admit that there is always some effect on film that is X-rayed, but sophisticated testing may be needed to reveal the precise extent. The results of X-rays show up first in the darkest areas of the photographic image after processing, and they take the form of shadows cast by X-ray absorbing objects that were adjacent to the film at the time of the test. The end caps of 35mm cassettes cast characteristic crescent shapes on the film and zips also leave an immediately recognizable pattern. The marks may appear in colour, since different layers of the film have different sensitivities to X-rays.

Fast film is affected first: though a single pass through an X-ray machine probably won't affect films rated at ISO 400 or slower, faster films should not be X-rayed at all. Tests by Fuji revealed that ISO 1600 colour print film showed damage after just one pass at 0.3mR (milliroentgens). ISO 400 film needed 10 passes, and ISO 100 film, 30 passes. The Federal Aviation Authority rules set an upper limit of 1 mR for X-ray baggage inspection, so even within the USA, the conservative may wish to divide Fuji's figures by 3. Some reports suggest that certain machines use X-ray dosages substantially higher than 1 mR. Speed alone does not determine the susceptibility of film to X-rays–colour films are more sensitive than monochrome and the orientation of the film within the machine significantly affects the damage done. The worst position for film is when the lips of the cassette are directed toward the X-ray beam, so as a last resort try to make sure the film does not go through with the cassettes orientated in this way.

Always ask for a hand search–in the USA at least, Federal Aviation Authority rules (number 108.17) state that everyone is entitled to a hand search if they request one. To make this easier, allow extra check-in time. Pack film cartons in a clear plastic bag to aid inspection and photocopy the following page to deter airport officials.

The magnetometer arch used to check for metal objects does not harm film–so offer to carry film through the arch if a hand search is refused.

X線厳禁

未現像フィルム在中

DO NOT
X-RAY

Contains Photographic Materials

BITTE NICHT
RÖNTGEN

Inhalt Fotomaterial

NE PAS
PASSER AUX
RAYONS X

Films Photo-sensibles

NO PASEN
POR
RAYOS X

Contiene Material Fotografico

厳禁X光透視

内装照相感光材料